OCCASIONAL PAPER 125

United Germany: The First Five Years

Performance and Policy Issues

Robert Corker, Robert A. Feldman, Karl Habermeier,
Hari Vittas, and Tessa van der Willigen

INTERNATIONAL MONETARY FUND
Washington DC
May 1995

Library of Congress Cataloging-in-Publication Data

United Germany the first five years : performance and policy issues /
  Robert Corker . . . [et al.].
     p. cm. — (Occasional Paper ; 125)
    Includes bibliographical references.
    ISBN 1-55775-472-1
    1. Germany—Economic policy—1990– 2. Germany—Economic
conditions—1990– 3. Germany—History—Unification, 1990.
I. Corker, Robert. II. Series: Occasional paper (International
Monetary Fund) ; no. 125.
HC286.8.U54 1995
338.943—dc20   95-18140
                                              CIP

Price: US$15.00
(US$12.00 to full-time faculty members and
students at universities and colleges)

Please send orders to:
International Monetary Fund, Publication Services
700 19th Street, N.W., Washington, D.C. 20431, U.S.A.
Tel.: (202) 623-7430   Telefax: (202) 623-7201
Internet: publications@imf.org

recycled paper

Contents

Charts

The following symbols have been used throughout this paper:

... to indicate that data are not available;

— to indicate that the figure is zero or less than half the final digit shown, or that the item does not exist;

– between years or months (e.g., 1991–92 or January–June) to indicate the years or months covered, including the beginning and ending years or months;

/ between years (e.g., 1991/92) to indicate a crop or fiscal (financial) year.

"Billion" means a thousand million.

Minor discrepancies between constituent figures and totals are due to rounding.

The term "country," as used in this paper, does not in all cases refer to a territorial entity that is a state as understood by international law and practice; the term also covers some territorial entities that are not states, but for which statistical data are maintained and provided internationally on a separate and independent basis.

Preface

This Occasional Paper reviews the progress of the German economy five years after unification and highlights some of the ongoing challenges it faces. The paper draws mainly from background work carried out in connection with the IMF staff's Article IV consultation discussions with the German authorities over the past two years. The staff teams for these discussions were led by Jacques R. Artus, whose insightful comments on this paper are gratefully acknowledged. The paper has also benefited substantially from stimulating discussions with German officials held at various government ministries in Bonn and at the Bundesbank, as well as their assistance in providing data and background material.

There are many individuals who have assisted in the production of this paper or who have offered valuable comments. In particular, the authors would like to thank Steven Symansky for running MULTIMOD simulations; Jolanta Stefanska for her superb research assistance in marshalling copious data; Kristy Pettie for extensive administrative and secretarial support; and Rozlyn Coleman for editing the paper for publication and coordinating production.

The views expressed here, as well as any errors, are the sole responsibility of the authors and do not necessarily reflect the opinions of the German Government, the Executive Directors of the IMF, or other members of the IMF staff.

The paper mainly reflects information available through August 1994, although in some cases it proved possible to insert more recent information.

1 Introduction

Hari Vittas

The purposes of this Occasional Paper are twofold: first, to review economic and financial developments in Germany since its reunification nearly five years ago; and, second, to analyze some critical issues that have featured prominently in the policy debate over this period and are likely to continue attracting attention in the years ahead.

Germany at a Glance

Total area	357,041 sq. kilometers
Total population	81.1 million
GNP per capita	$23,203
West Germany	$26,088
East Germany	$11,117

The discussion of economic developments is organized in many instances along regional lines. This is mainly because regional trends have shown large and persistent divergences, which have been of interest from a policy perspective. It needs to be stressed, however, that this separation is increasingly difficult to sustain statistically and is also less and less appropriate as the two parts of Germany become more fully integrated. Moreover, notwithstanding their divergence, the early postunification trends in east and west Germany have had some common causes. In particular, the large fiscal transfers from west to east, which have been instrumental in generating economic recovery in the new states of the Federal Republic, have also contributed markedly to the emergence of inflationary pressures and the subsequent recession in the old states.

Domestic Economic Developments

West Germany has experienced wide swings in economic activity since unification. These have reflected to some extent the effects of fluctuations in the international business cycle. More important, though, they have been influenced by the unexpectedly large costs of supporting incomes in and rebuilding the economy of the former German Democratic Republic, as well as the policies adopted to cope with the resulting strains on macroeconomic performance and the public finances. Initially, transfers to east Germany were financed entirely through borrowing. The implied large fiscal expansion boosted demand at a time when the economy was already close to overheating. As a result, economic growth accelerated noticeably from an average of 3½ percent in 1988–89 to nearly 6 percent in 1990 (Table 1-1). Inevitably, however, pressures on resources also became acute, and both wage and price inflation escalated rapidly.

Subsequently, monetary policy was tightened in an effort to curb inflationary pressures, and action was initiated to reduce the fiscal deficit. Concurrently, foreign demand weakened. In response to these developments, the postunification boom gradually tapered off and gave way from mid-1992 to a deep recession. The recession was concentrated in the manufacturing sector and reached its trough in the first quarter of 1993, when real GDP was some 3 percent lower than a year earlier and industrial production was as much as 10 percent below its peak (Chart 1-1). It was accompanied by a large fall in employment as the effects of the decline in output were exacerbated by labor-saving restructuring, particularly in export-oriented industries.

With the growing slack in labor and output markets, inflationary pressures gradually receded. In particular, the increase in wage earnings decelerated sharply from an average of 6 to 7 percent in 1991–92 to 4 percent in 1993 and further to about 2 percent in 1994. The slowdown in the growth of unit labor costs was even more pronounced because of the large productivity gains associated with the cyclical recovery in output and labor shedding in the manufacturing sector. Consumer price inflation proved more resilient, mainly because of increases in indirect taxes, local authorities' charges, and the cost of housing. Nevertheless, it too has been on a downward trend since late 1992, enabling the Bundesbank to allow monetary conditions to ease progressively.

The relaxation of monetary conditions, coupled with a gradual strengthening of foreign demand, provided the basis for a revival of economic activity.

Table 1-1. Main Economic Indicators

	1990[1]	1991	1992	1993	1994[2]
	(Percentage changes)				
GDP at 1991 prices	5.8	2.8	2.2	−1.1	2.8
Total domestic demand	5.2	6.1	3.0	−1.2	2.7
Exports of goods and nonfactor services	11.3	−2.2	0.2	−6.2	6.8
Imports of goods and nonfactor services	10.2	11.2	3.3	−6.1	6.2
Employment and unemployment					
Employment	3.0	−2.1	−1.6	−1.8	−0.9
Unemployed in percent of labor force	6.2	6.6	7.7	8.8	9.6
Prices					
GDP deflator	3.1	5.0	5.5	3.9	2.2
Consumer prices index	2.7	4.6	4.9	4.7	3.1
	(In percent of GDP)				
Public finances[3]					
General government					
Expenditure	42.3	48.9	49.3	50.4	50.0
Revenue	40.4	45.7	46.8	47.1	47.5
Financial balance	−1.9	−3.2	−2.6	−3.3	−2.4
Borrowing requirement of the Treuhand	0.2	0.7	0.9	1.2	1.1
General government debt	39.8	41.1	43.7	47.7	51.0
Balance of payments[4]					
Current account	2.9	−1.1	−1.1	−1.0	−1.1
Trade balance[5]	4.4	1.4	1.6	2.3	2.5
	(Percent changes)				
Monetary data (annual averages)[6]					
Money and quasi–money (M3)	13.5	10.7	8.5	8.2	8.5
Domestic bank lending	11.8	11.9	10.6	9.8	9.5
	(Annual averages in percent)				
Interest rates					
Three-month money market rate	8.6	9.2	9.5	7.2	5.3
Yield on government bonds	8.9	8.6	8.0	6.3	6.7
	(Levels)				
Exchange rates					
DM per US$ (annual average)	1.62	1.66	1.56	1.65	1.62
Nominal effective rate (1990=100)	100.0	99.1	102.1	106.1	106.4
Real effective rate (1990=100)	100.0	98.7	100.9	108.3	106.8
	(Percentage changes)				
West Germany					
GDP at 1991 prices	5.8	4.9	1.8	−1.7	2.3
Total domestic demand	5.2	4.9	1.3	−2.2	1.9
Exports of goods and nonfactor services	11.3	10.6	5.4	−3.2	7.4
Imports of goods and nonfactor services	10.2	11.6	4.4	−5.3	7.2
Manufacturing output	5.5	3.2	−2.1	−7.7	3.4
Employment and unemployment					
Employment	3.0	2.6	0.9	−1.6	−1.3
Unemployed in percent of labor force	6.2	5.5	5.8	7.3	8.3
Prices and earnings					
GDP deflator	3.1	4.0	4.4	3.2	2.1
Consumer price index	2.7	3.5	4.0	4.1	3.0
Average hourly earnings (industry)	5.7	7.3	7.1	6.1	1.3
Unit labor costs (total economy)	2.0	3.6	5.0	3.5	−1.1

(continued)

Table 1-1 *(concluded)*

	1990	1991	1992	1993	1994[2]
			(Percentage changes)		
East Germany					
GDP at 1991 prices	...	–18.7	7.8	5.8	8.9
Total domestic demand	...	15.7	15.0	5.4	7.5
Exports of goods and nonfactor services	...	32.3	10.3	5.5	22.6
Imports of goods and nonfactor services	...	117.2	21.3	5.0	9.4
Manufacturing output	...	...	–2.7	9.0	21.7
Employment and unemployment					
Employment	...	–17.1	–11.7	–2.9	0.8
Unemployed in percent of labor force	2.9	10.7	14.7	14.8	14.6
Prices and earnings					
GDP deflator	...	16.6	18.2	9.9	2.4
Consumer price index	...	...	11.1	8.9	3.3
Average hourly earnings (industry)	...	...	26.2	14.1	8.2
Unit labor costs (total economy)	...	35.1	10.9	2.5	0.2

Sources: Deutsche Bundesbank, *Monthly Report* (various issues); Statistisches Bundesamt, Volkswirtschaftliche Gesamtrechnungen; and IMF staff estimates.

[1]Data for GDP and components, employment, unemployment, and prices refer to west Germany.

[2]Preliminary estimates.

[3]Data for general government are on national accounts basis and incorporate east Germany from 1991. Debt data are end-of-year and include the German Unity Fund and east Germany from 1990.

[4]West Germany until June 1990.

[5]Including supplementary trade items.

[6]Monetary data include east Germany from end-June 1990, thereby distorting growth rates in both 1990 and 1991.

This was set in motion during 1993 but gathered significant momentum only in 1994, by which time many of the initial tensions created by unification had been overcome and both business and consumer confidence had recovered strongly. As in previous cyclical upturns, the revival in activity was led by a strong rebound in exports and was supported, after a lag, by a gradual pickup in business investment. With consumer spending also showing surprising resilience, in the face of declining real household disposable income, real GDP grew by an estimated 2¼ percent in 1994, reversing most of its decline during the recession. Employment growth, however, was slow to respond to the upturn in economic activity, and the unemployment rate remained close to its historical peak of 8¼ percent through the end of 1994. With output still well below potential and wage increases remaining subdued, the rate of inflation continued to decline.

In east Germany, real GDP fell by no less than one fourth in the 18 months to the end of 1991 (Chart 1-2). The fall in manufacturing output was even steeper, reflecting the collapse of traditional export markets in the former socialist bloc and a shift in consumer preferences toward higher-quality products imported from the west. The contraction in the production base of the new eastern Länder precipitated a sharp decline in employment. Despite substantial emigration to the west and the adoption of large-scale retraining and early retirement schemes, unemployment skyrocketed to over 1 million, or 15 percent of the dependent labor force, while the number of people in short-time work or job creation programs also rose markedly. Meanwhile, the rate of inflation shot up as prices began to converge to those in west Germany.

The decline in output came to a halt during the course of 1991 and has since been followed by a rapid expansion. This was at first concentrated in the nontradable sectors—construction and services—which benefited from the increased demand generated by the transfers from west Germany. But manufacturing too began to show signs of revival in late 1992. These became more clearly visible in 1993 and 1994, when output expanded by 6 percent and 9 percent, respectively. It is worth noting, however, that despite its robust growth over the past two years, net manufacturing output remains about one fourth lower than it was before unification. Moreover, little progress has been made so far in revers-

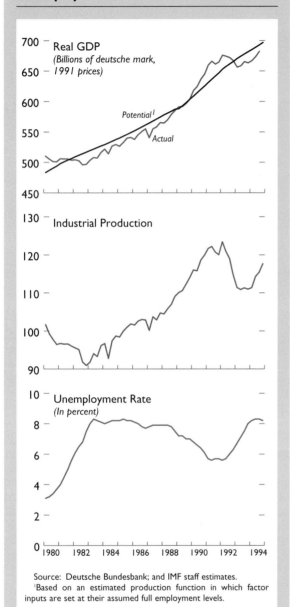

Chart 1-1. West Germany: Output and Unemployment

Source: Deutsche Bundesbank; and IMF staff estimates.
[1]Based on an estimated production function in which factor inputs are set at their assumed full employment levels.

Chart 1-2. East Germany: Output and Employment

Sources: Statistisches Bundesamt, *Volkswirtschaftliche Gesamtrechnungen*; and Deutsche Bundesbank, *Monthly Report*.
[1]Seasonally adjusted.

Balance of Payments

The unification boom brought about a large shift in the pattern of saving and investment in Germany. The main features of the shift were a surge of investment activity in the new states, which led to a sizable increase in the investment ratio and a sharp drop in national savings, which was to a large extent accounted for by the deterioration in the public finances. The counterpart of these changes in saving and investment was a turnaround in the current account of the balance of payments from a sizable surplus (in west Germany), averaging more than 4 percent of GDP in the late 1980s, to a deficit of about 1 percent (in all of Germany) in 1991–92 (Chart 1-3). The emergence of the deficit was, at first, mainly a consequence of the excessive pressures on domestic resources, which boosted the demand for imports while simultaneously contributing to a diversion of some of west Germany's exports to east Germany. Subsequently, a loss of competitiveness, resulting from Germany's comparatively high rate of domestic inflation in 1991–93 and the steep nominal effective apprecia-

ing the large reduction in employment experienced during the early 1990s, and the unemployment rate is still about 14 percent. On the other hand, the pace of wage convergence slowed and the rate of inflation decelerated progressively, as the price level approached that in the west. In fact, by the beginning of 1995 the east German rate of increase in consumer prices had fallen somewhat below that in west Germany.

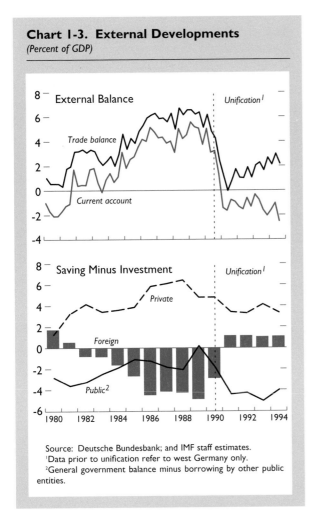

Chart 1-3. External Developments
(Percent of GDP)

Source: Deutsche Bundesbank; and IMF staff estimates.
[1]Data prior to unification refer to west Germany only.
[2]General government balance minus borrowing by other public entities.

have recourse to foreign savings to finance the rebuilding of the east German economy.

Developments in the capital account of the balance of payments and in external reserves were dominated by the large swings in speculative flows around the time of the 1992–93 crises in the European exchange rate mechanism (ERM). In addition, changes in the tax treatment of interest income had at times a significant impact on portfolio investment and the foreign position of the banking sector. On balance, Germany experienced a modest capital inflow over the 1990–94 period, which was sufficient to finance its current account deficit as well as a small buildup of official external reserves.

Financial Policies

Fiscal developments in the early 1990s have been dominated by the large budgetary and extrabudgetary transfers to east Germany. These turned out to be far greater than initially expected, averaging well over 4 percent of total German GDP in the four years to 1994. From a position of broad balance in 1989, the general government accounts deteriorated markedly to show a deficit of more than 3 percent of GDP in 1991, notwithstanding the strong boost to revenues from the overheating economy. In addition, borrowing by other public entities, including the Treuhandanstalt, rose rapidly to exceed 1 percent of GDP by 1991.

A first phase of adjustment (entailing mainly a temporary income tax surcharge and a 1 percentage point increase in the standard value-added tax rate) was initiated in 1992, but its impact coincided with powerful offsetting effects of the automatic stabilizers. As a result, the general government deficit did not show much of a fall, while borrowing by other public sector entities rose further to 1½ percent of GDP in 1993.

In early 1993, agreement was reached on a second phase of fiscal adjustment, in the form of a "Solidarity Pact" between the federal and the state governments and the opposition parties. The pact provided for new arrangements for revenue sharing between the Federal Government and the local authorities and included a package of measures to be implemented over the medium term with a view to restoring a sound fiscal position. This package of consolidation measures was subsequently strengthened by the Government, and the bulk of it was enacted by the end of 1993. Key elements of the package were the reimposition of a 7½ percent solidarity surcharge on income tax obligations effective in 1995, a reduction in unemployment benefits as of 1994, and an increase in the fuel tax in 1994 with the proceeds to be used to finance a reform of the railways. In addi-

tion of the deutsche mark (especially during the European exchange rate crises of 1992–93), helped to sustain the deficit. The trade position strengthened somewhat in 1992–93 owing mainly to favorable cyclical effects, but there was an offsetting deterioration in the invisibles balance, which reflected in part a sharp reduction in net investment income from abroad.

In 1994, Germany experienced a significant recovery in its competitive position. Domestic unit labor costs actually declined as a very modest rise in wage earnings was accompanied by exceptionally large productivity gains. At the same time, the upward trend in the nominal effective exchange rate of the deutsche mark was interrupted. The improvement in competitiveness, in combination with the strong cyclical rebound in foreign demand, helped to strengthen the trade balance. However, the current account deficit remained about 1 percent of GDP as net investment income from abroad continued to decline. Thus, in a small way, Germany continued to

tion, several steps were taken to streamline family assistance programs, to cut other discretionary spending, and to reduce tax shelters and loopholes. Partly as a result of the implementation of some of these measures, the general government deficit declined to 2½ percent of GDP in 1994 and is set to fall further over the next two years, notwithstanding the rebudgetization of outlays (such as the servicing of Treuhand and railway debt) that hitherto had been off budget.

Thus, within a relatively short period of time, Germany has made major progress in redressing the fiscal imbalances created by the costs of unification and is already satisfying the fiscal convergence criteria of the Maastricht Treaty. An important drawback, however, is that the fiscal consolidation has been achieved at the cost of a significant increase in the overall tax burden (Chart 1-4). This has weakened economic incentives and risks depressing the economy's potential over the medium term and undermining Germany's attractiveness as a location for investment and production. This risk is well recognized by the authorities. Indeed, lowering the tax burden is high on the Government's agenda for the current legislative period (1995–98). However, the means of achieving this objective, and the requisite expenditure cutbacks, have not yet been spelled out in detail.

The fiscal strains and overheating attendant upon unification led the Bundesbank to move firmly to tighten monetary conditions. Official interest rates were raised repeatedly from early 1990 to August 1992 to peak at close to 9–10 percent. Money market rates moved in concert with official rates. Thus, by August 1992, the three-month interbank rate had risen to 9.8 percent, compared with about 8 percent at the beginning of 1990. Subsequently, inflationary pressures abated and the Bundesbank was able to allow monetary conditions to ease. The process of easing was gradual and at times interrupted by a perceived need to reassure financial markets, as well as participants in the wage bargaining process, that the authorities continued to attach the highest priority to restoring price stability. Nevertheless, by mid-1994, official rates had fallen about 5 percentage points below their 1992 peaks while market rates followed a broadly similar path. Thereafter, official rates remained virtually unchanged but market rates firmed somewhat as the recovery in economic activity gathered strength.

Bond yields rose sharply during the first half of 1990 as the markets anticipated that unification would increase inflationary pressures and the demand for capital to finance reconstruction in east Germany. After unification, however, yields began to fall, notwithstanding the massive recourse by the public sector to the bond market and the progressive

Chart 1-4. General Government Finances[1]
(In percent of GDP)

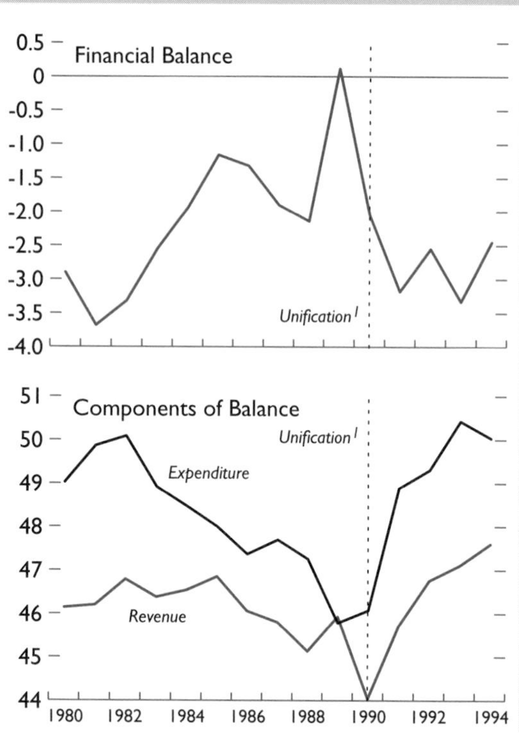

Sources: Federal Ministry of Finance; and IMF staff projections.
[1]Data prior to unification refer to west Germany only.

acceleration of inflation. The fall was at first gentle and appears to have reflected mainly the downward trend in bond yields abroad, which increased the relative attractiveness of German securities. Since the end of 1991, however, the decline in the return on German bonds accelerated as investors became increasingly confident that the Bundesbank would succeed in its efforts to safeguard the domestic and external stability of the currency. Thus, the yield curve, which had been inverted since 1991, steepened considerably. Bond yields reached a low of 5.5 percent in January 1994 and have since increased by 2 percentage points, contributing to a normalization of the yield curve. The increase, however, was considerably less pronounced in Germany than in most other industrial countries. This tends to support the view that it reflected the effects of the worldwide buoyancy of economic activity and investment rather than any concerns about a rekindling of domestic inflationary pressures.

The evolution of the monetary aggregates in the postunification period has become difficult to interpret. This reflects both uncertainties about the properties of money demand in east Germany and temporary distortions associated with the currency crises in the ERM and changes in the tax treatment of interest income. Notwithstanding these difficulties, the Bundesbank has retained the practice of announcing target ranges for the growth in M3 deemed consistent with its objective of lowering inflation to no more than 2 percent over the medium term. However, in the face of the aforementioned distortions in monetary behavior, it showed flexibility in pursuing its targets. Indeed, the growth of M3 was allowed to exceed the upper bound of its target range by a significant margin in each of the three years to 1993. Overshooting of the target range continued in the early months of 1994, but subsequently M3 virtually ceased to grow and by the end of the year it was within the target range (Chart 1-5).

Structural Reform

Since unification, the German economy has also undergone a profound structural transformation. The most sweeping changes have occurred in eastern Germany, where the bulk of the state-owned enterprises has been placed in private hands and massive infrastructure investment has been undertaken, laying the foundation for economic convergence with the west. In western Germany, the deep recession forced industrial enterprises to increase productivity in an environment of high costs and mounting international competition. The industrial shakeout was mirrored in the policy debate, which began to focus on keeping Germany attractive as a location for investment. There has also been a rethinking of the proper division of labor between the private and public sectors, and the switches have been set for an eventual privatization of the railways and the state-owned postal and telecommunications companies.

Outline of Paper

The remainder of this paper is organized as follows. Chapter II takes up the issue of whether the appreciation of the deutsche mark in recent years and the rise in labor costs have had a significant adverse effect on the competitiveness of the German economy and its export performance. It examines various measures of competitiveness, including conventional indicators and some that are less widely used. The chapter finds that the deterioration in Germany's external competitiveness has almost certainly been exaggerated by standard indicators, such as relative unit labor costs in manufacturing, and that

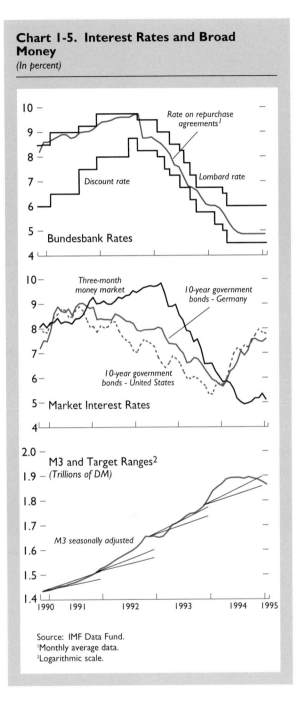

Chart 1-5. Interest Rates and Broad Money
(In percent)

Rate on repurchase agreements[1]

Discount rate

Lombard rate

Bundesbank Rates

Three-month money market

10-year government bonds - Germany

10-year government bonds - United States

Market Interest Rates

M3 and Target Ranges[2]
(Trillions of DM)

M3 seasonally adjusted

1990 1991 1992 1993 1994 1995

Source: IMF Data Fund.
[1]Monthly average data.
[2]Logarithmic scale.

recent export performance and the export outlook do not appear to have been seriously impaired.

Chapter III examines the link between high unemployment and labor market institutions in Germany. It argues that labor markets in Germany have become increasingly segmented between high- and low-productivity workers and that only a small part of the unemployment problem is cyclical in origin. Reform of income support for the unemployed, a re-examination of social assistance, and some relaxation of employment protection could facilitate the reintegration of lower-skilled workers into the economy.

Chapter IV analyzes the relationship between economic growth, on the one hand, and the size of the public sector and the tax burden, on the other. In addition, this chapter uses the IMF's MULTIMOD economic model to explore the macroeconomic effects of changes in the structure of the public finances. The results suggest that a reduction in the size of the public sector may be beneficial, as may a lesser reliance on wage taxes.

Chapter V presents an empirical analysis of different monetary indicators in order to shed some light on the issue of whether the overshooting of the broad money supply target in recent years raises the specter of a renewed acceleration of inflation. The analysis suggests that in the period preceding unification a monetary conditions index (MCI), constructed as a weighted average of real short-term interest rates and the real effective exchange rate, would have provided useful early warning signals for inflation, broadly similar to those emanating from the behavior of broad money. However, neither indicator would have predicted developments in inflation around the turn of the decade very well. This is perhaps not a surprising result given the unprecedented nature of the demand shock to the west German economy associated with unification.

More interesting is the finding that during 1992–93, when money growth increased significantly, the MCI indicated that monetary conditions remained fairly tight. Since there were good reasons to suspect that the monetary data were distorted by special factors, the behavior of the MCI at this time suggests that the policy of cutting official interest rates during 1993 and the first half of 1994, even in the face of further surges in monetary growth, was appropriate. The validity of this policy is also borne out by the subsequent slowdown in monetary growth in the second half of 1994 and the favorable evolution of wage and price inflation.

Finally, Chapter VI investigates the prospects for self-sustaining growth in eastern Germany. This subject has important ramifications for economic performance in Germany as a whole—including the public finances and the balance of payments. Following an analytical overview of the principal forces likely to sustain or impede economic growth in the east, the chapter develops a two-sector growth model that links investment, the labor market, and technological change. This framework is used to assess the evolution of potential output in eastern Germany and to gauge the effect of excessive wages on the demand for labor. The simulations show that the economy is likely to expand at a rapid rate for a number of years but that the large imbalance in the labor market poses a risk to this outlook.

II External Competitiveness[1]

Robert A. Feldman

This chapter assesses Germany's external competitiveness through the summer of 1994. This issue is particularly interesting in light of the substantial real appreciation of the deutsche mark in recent years suggested by several conventional indicators of the real exchange rate and the key role that exports have played in past economic recoveries. It is worth noting at the outset that the concept of external competitiveness is a multidimensional one, which, at the macroeconomic level, cannot be adequately captured in a single measure. Indices of the real exchange rate provide a useful guide, but an array of other factors that do not lend themselves to direct quantification also affects competitiveness, including reliability, quality, after-sales service, delivery times, financing arrangements, technological innovation, and the like.

It is also worth emphasizing that an observed change in an index of the real exchange rate may simply represent an equilibrium response to changed economic circumstances, in which case any resulting deterioration in net exports would not necessarily be a cause for concern. Consider a recent example: some real appreciation of the deutsche mark was to be expected in the wake of unification as an endogenous equilibrating response to the capital needs and demands of the former east Germany. This response served to divert west German exports from foreign markets to a buoyant east German market and to encourage higher imports in order to meet increased domestic demand. Thus by itself the appreciation did not represent a competitiveness problem.[2]

A key conclusion of this chapter is that the deterioration of Germany's external competitiveness suggested by some commonly used indicators of the real appreciation of the deutsche mark, such as those based on relative unit labor costs in manufacturing, is almost certainly exaggerated. By implication, the concern sometimes expressed that Germany's ability to compete internationally may have been impaired by an appreciating real exchange rate, to such an extent as to undermine prospects for sustainable recovery, can be viewed as largely unfounded.

The assessment of competitiveness is carried out from several angles. The next section discusses movements in several real exchange rate indices for Germany and reviews briefly their relationship to observed changes in trade flows. With this as background, the chapter then moves on to assess developments in competitiveness using the so-called constant market share approach. This approach essentially entails a decomposition of German export growth into four components: a global market growth effect; a commodity composition effect; a market distribution effect; and a residual "competitiveness" effect. The latter can be interpreted as an indication of Germany's ability, for any number of reasons, to compete effectively with other sources of supply. The extent to which international competition may have narrowed German profit margins in tradable goods is also investigated. The chapter concludes with an assessment of trade prospects based in part on recent developments in export order statistics.[3]

[1]The author would like to thank Jacques R. Artus, Peter Clark, Robert Corker, Mohsin Khan, Manmohan Kumar, Tessa van der Willigen, and Harilaos Vittas for helpful discussions and suggestions. Aarne Dimanlig, Toh Kuan, Susana Mursula, and Rosa Vera-Bunge provided valuable research assistance.

[2]See Masson and Meredith (1990) and Adams, Alexander, and Gagnon (1992). It might be noted that the analysis in both of these papers suggests that some real depreciation of the deutsche mark would later be prompted by the withdrawal of stimulus related to the earlier unification shock.

[3]It is evident that measures of international competitiveness by themselves cannot be taken as measures of economic well-being and that the goal of economic policy is not to achieve a particular target for performance in the traded goods sector. Rather, policies should be aimed directly at promoting appropriately high and sustainable rates of saving and investment, correspondingly high productivity and economic growth, and thereby an improved standard of living—factors that may also have a positive impact on a country's ability to compete in international markets. Several articles by Paul Krugman discuss the misuse of the notion of international competitiveness as an underlying reason for economic difficulties that are primarily domestic in origin. Just three examples are Krugman (1994a, 1994b, and 1991).

Developments in Real Exchange Rate Indices

Manufacturing Sector

Chart 2-1 plots various real effective exchange rate indices for the manufacturing sector, all of which point to a significant loss of competitiveness between 1985 and mid-1990, the latter point being the eve of unification (July 1990). Part of this loss of competitiveness can be viewed as the counterpart of the correction of the U.S. dollar, which, as is widely recognized, was significantly overvalued in the mid-1980s. However, even if the period surrounding the dollar's overvaluation is taken to be somewhat abnormal, the indicators still show a sizable deterioration in German competitiveness, and this is true whether one compares exchange rate indices in mid-1990 with the late 1970s, 1980, or 1987.

Developments in the various indicators in the later part of the 1980s suggest at first sight that exporters may have responded to the appreciating deutsche mark and rising unit labor costs by reducing their profit margins (at least relative to those in competitor countries) in an effort to hold on to market share.[4] The indices shown in Charts 2-1 and 2-2 do indeed start to diverge considerably in 1987 and show significant cumulative differences by mid-1990. By then, the index of the relative unit labor costs was roughly 10 percent higher than that of the nominal effective exchange rate. By contrast, the relative export price index actually declined from its end-1986 level, after having broadly kept pace with the other indices.[5]

However, it would be erroneous to interpret the apparent decline in Germany's relative export profit margins as indicative of a genuine profit squeeze. During most of the period preceding unification, there was a tendency in many industrial countries, particularly in Europe, for income distribution to

shift from labor to capital. Both the rate of return on capital and the capital income share in the business sector were at historically high levels in Germany at the beginning of the 1990s, after rising steadily dur-

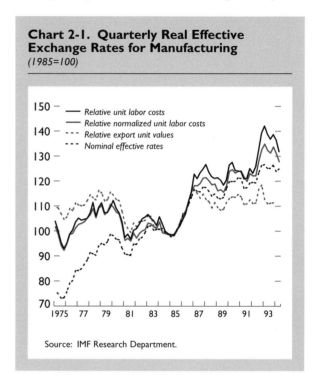

Chart 2-1. Quarterly Real Effective Exchange Rates for Manufacturing
(1985=100)

- Relative unit labor costs
- Relative normalized unit labor costs
- Relative export unit values
- Nominal effective rates

Source: IMF Research Department.

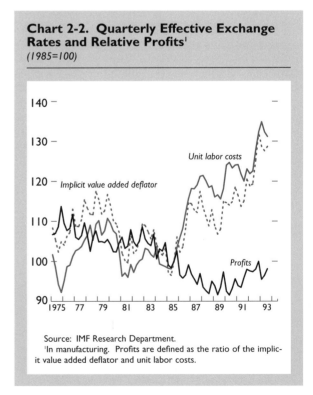

Chart 2-2. Quarterly Effective Exchange Rates and Relative Profits[1]
(1985=100)

Unit labor costs

Implicit value added deflator

Profits

Source: IMF Research Department.
[1]In manufacturing. Profits are defined as the ratio of the implicit value added deflator and unit labor costs.

---

[4]The strategy of defending market share through squeezing profits is not one that can be sustained in the long run—thus the argument that indicators based on relative costs, whether unit labor costs or more comprehensive measures of costs discussed later, are particularly relevant for assessing external competitiveness from a longer-term perspective.

[5]Lipschitz and McDonald (1991) offer evidence that profit margins in the ERM countries increased relative to those in Germany up to 1988.

It is important to note that the later part of the 1980s witnessed a large fall in the price of oil. While this would have benefited both domestic and foreign exporters' profit margins, the benefit to Germany was probably more pronounced because of greater reliance on imported oil than many other industrial countries. Nevertheless, comparing the index based on unit labor costs to one based on value-added deflators in manufacturing, instead of export unit values, still indicates declining relative profit margins, particularly later in the 1980s (Chart 2-2).

ing the 1980s. Data on profit margins for the German enterprise sector, particularly for the manufacturing sector, indicate that profits fell perceptibly in 1991 for the first time since the beginning of the upswing at the end of 1982.[6]

From unification to mid-1993, there was a further real appreciation of the deutsche mark, in terms of relative unit labor costs, of about 10 percent, with virtually all of this appreciation being accounted for in the last year of this period. An appreciation of the nominal effective exchange rate was important, but more rapid growth of unit labor costs in Germany than in her competitor countries also contributed. Since mid-1993, there has been some easing back of the real effective deutsche mark (in terms of relative unit labor costs) from its earlier peak (Chart 2-1).

Broader-Based Indices[7]

Although measures of unit labor costs in manufacturing reveal important information about production costs for a sector that accounts for a large proportion of merchandise exports and imports (manufactured goods accounted for almost 97 percent of west German exports and almost 88 percent of its imports in 1992), caution needs to be exercised when interpreting unit labor costs as a measure of competitiveness. In particular, there are significant problems with available data on unit labor costs in manufacturing. These data encompass only the costs of labor services that are incurred directly in manufacturing and therefore exclude the costs of other important labor inputs that are used in producing manufactured goods. These excluded costs may take the form of labor from the services sector—for example, legal or marketing services if these are not performed in-house—as well as other indirect labor costs embodied in the intermediate inputs needed for producing manufactures. Such labor costs can have an important effect on the cost of manufactured goods produced in Germany relative to competitor countries and therefore need to be recognized in the analysis. Labor costs in manufacturing account directly for a much smaller fraction of total production costs.[8] In addition, there may be problems of inter-

national comparability in the definitions of the manufacturing sector, problems that lead to differences in the extent to which certain suppliers and service areas are included in the manufacturing sector across countries. Such comparability problems may be reflected in the fact that measured unit labor costs in German manufacturing have recorded larger increases than unit labor costs in other business sectors, whereas in most competitor countries sectoral differences in the evolution of unit labor costs have been the reverse.[9]

In light of the discussion above, it seems sensible to examine relative unit labor costs from the broader perspective of the overall business sector. Of course, this does not solve all problems: the costs of other important inputs that affect relative cost competitiveness, such as the costs of various capital inputs, are still not taken into account. Moreover, the business sector covers not only the tradables sector but also parts of the economy that are sheltered from foreign competition. Nevertheless, the broader indicators add another dimension to the analysis by trying to account for the fact that competitiveness in German manufacturing also depends on labor inputs provided by other parts of the German economy. Moreover, the definitional problems for the manufacturing sector should not be as important.

As with indicators based on the manufacturing sector alone, more broadly based indicators show an appreciation of the real effective exchange rate (Chart 2-3). The various indices peak in 1993 and then reverse to some degree in the more recent quarters, reflecting increases in labor productivity, moderate wage settlements, and some modest depreciation of the deutsche mark. What is striking, however, is that the levels of the broader-based indicators suggest a much smaller cumulative real appreciation of the deutsche mark since the mid-1980s than those for the manufacturing sector alone. In fact, relative unit labor costs for the business sector as a whole are estimated to have been slightly below their 1987 peak recently, in sharp contrast to the continued

---

[6]A later section contains further discussion of profit margins in Germany.

[7]Much of this section draws on Deutsche Bundesbank (1994b, pp. 45–57).

[8]To emphasize this point, the Bundesbank notes, "Although labor costs—in terms of the value added—constitute by far the most significant cost factor in the manufacturing sector, with a share of 70 percent, in relation to the total value of the finished product (in other words, including the intermediate work undertaken by other domestic sectors and by sectors abroad), the labor costs incurred directly in manufacturing account for only about one-quarter of the total." See Deutsche Bundesbank (1994b, p. 51).

[9]As is well known, there are other difficulties associated with using data on unit labor costs. Changes in the prices of inputs other than labor affect competitiveness but are not captured by examining unit labor costs alone. For example, the substitution of capital for labor may result in a lower unit labor cost index but higher capital costs, so the decline in unit labor costs overstates any improvement in cost competitiveness. In the process, labor may be reduced, and, more important, some marginal activities, typically where productivity is relatively low, would cease altogether. It may, in fact, be a lack of competitiveness that causes the output of tradables to fall, but that also results in a rise in average productivity. More detailed discussion of these difficulties, as well as more general difficulties with measures of real exchange rates, is found in Lipschitz and McDonald (1991), Turner and Van't dack (1993), Wickham (1993), and Marsh and Tokarick (1994).

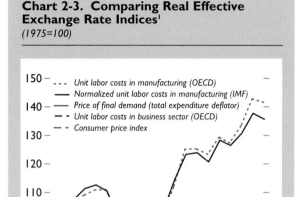

Chart 2-3. Comparing Real Effective Exchange Rate Indices[1]
(1975=100)

- - - - Unit labor costs in manufacturing (OECD)
——— Normalized unit labor costs in manufacturing (IMF)
——— Price of final demand (total expenditure deflator)
- - Unit labor costs in business sector (OECD)
- - Consumer price index

Source: Deutsche Bundesbank (1994b); and IMF Research Department.
[1]Weighted real external value of the deutsche mark against currencies of 18 industrial countries (external value of the basis of unit labor cost in the manufacturing sector without Greece and Ireland). For 1994, data for the first quarter are shown.

steep rise during this period suggested by the index of relative unit labor costs in manufacturing alone. This implies that the growth in relative unit labor costs in the nonmanufacturing sectors has been much more subdued than in manufacturing itself; and, to the extent that inputs from the former are used in producing manufactured goods, German competitiveness would be stronger than suggested by relative unit labor costs in the manufacturing sector alone.

Furthermore, there is evidence that relative unit labor costs for the business sector as a whole are more closely correlated empirically with the observed behavior of exports. For example, the Bundesbank, in a May 1994 study, uses a simple regression framework to obtain an estimated elasticity of exports with respect to unit labor costs in the business sector of –0.22 in the short run and –0.36 in the long run; both are statistically significant. By contrast, similar elasticities for unit labor costs in manufacturing are not significant (–0.14 and –0.21 in the short and long runs, respectively).

The other indicators based on total expenditure deflators and consumer prices have tended to move fairly closely with relative unit labor costs for the business sector over the past 20 years; thus, they

also stand well below the manufacturing indices. However, while these variables are also statistically significant in export equations, they do not explain exports as well as relative unit labor costs.[10] Like unit labor costs, the index based on expenditure deflators can be interpreted as an indicator of costs per unit of output; but in this case it covers total costs, which include the prices of all factors of production and, therefore, supplement and extend the information based on unit labor costs. Such broad-based indices can also reflect the ratio of the relative prices of nontradable goods to tradable goods at home and abroad: an increase in this index would reflect either a loss of competitiveness in the traded goods market or a greater incentive to allocate resources to the nontradable goods sector at home than abroad.[11]

To extend the analysis, it is instructive to consider directly the price of nontradables relative to tradables, another measure of international competitiveness, which is often referred to in the literature as the real (or internal real) exchange rate. This measure also recognizes the important fact that a country's international performance depends on developments in the nontradables sector. If the real exchange rate appreciates—that is, the price of nontradables rises relative to the price of tradables—resources will tend to be reallocated away from the tradable goods sector, with the trade balance deteriorating accordingly; in this sense, competitiveness is said to worsen.[12] However, one problem is that this measure may not entail a loss of competitiveness (or may overstate such a loss), even when rising over time, if the growth in labor (or total factor) productivity differs across sectors of the economy.

The internal real exchange rate shows much less of an appreciation than the indices based on the manufacturing sector (Chart 2-4). And even here, the internal real exchange rate overstates the deterioration in actual competitiveness insofar as labor productivity (and total factor productivity) in the tradable goods sector has been rising more rapidly than

---

[10]Marsh and Tokarick (1994) suggest that export volume equations using competitiveness indicators based on unit labor costs (normalized) can explain trade flows for exports of goods overall, and for manufactured goods alone, somewhat better than indicators based on consumer prices or export unit values.

[11]If prices of traded goods in different countries are closely related through international competition, then a real appreciation of the currency as measured by aggregate price indices would suggest that developments in the internal terms of trade are more favorable to nontraded goods in the appreciating country.

[12]Underlying this adjustment is the idea that the internal real exchange rate represents the domestic cost of consuming and producing tradable goods and is a summary measure of the incentives guiding resource allocation between the two major sectors of the economy.

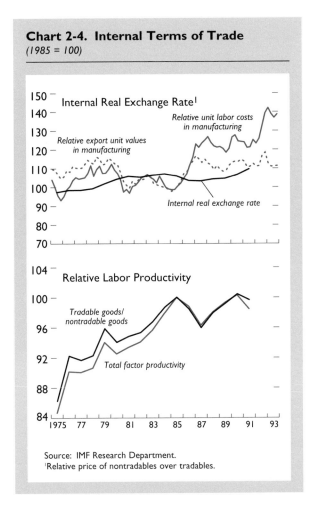

Chart 2-4. Internal Terms of Trade
(1985 = 100)

Internal Real Exchange Rate[1]

Relative unit labor costs in manufacturing

Relative export unit values in manufacturing

Internal real exchange rate

Relative Labor Productivity

Tradable goods/ nontradable goods

Total factor productivity

Source: IMF Research Department.
[1]Relative price of nontradables over tradables.

in the nontradable goods sector.[13] In addition, the effects of an appreciation of the internal real exchange rate on the trade balance could be lessened if similar trends occur in competitor countries.[14]

In summary, while conventional measures of Germany's real exchange rate, based on data for the manufacturing sector alone, point to a sizable loss of external competitiveness in the 1980s and early 1990s, this conclusion is much less apparent from an examination of more broadly based measures.

---

[13]The data used to construct these variables are available through 1991 and are from the OECD international sectoral data base, comprising 14 countries and 20 sectors. Tradables are defined to include those sectors in which more than 10 percent of total production for all 14 countries combined is exported. For details on this data base and classification, see De Gregorio, Giovannini, and Wolf (1994). The data used here update their calculations for 1970–85 up to 1991.

[14]De Gregorio, Giovannini, and Wolf (1994) provide evidence of the increase in the relative price of nontradables for 14 OECD countries, using the OECD international sectoral data base.

Trade Performance and Related Developments

This section begins with an analysis of export market shares to see if further light can be shed on the German competitiveness issue. This analysis suggests that a competitiveness problem has not been particularly evident in the actual performance of German exports. The section goes on to review the available data on developments in sectoral profits as another channel through which competitive pressures may have had an impact.

Constant Market Share Analysis

Constant market share analysis takes into account the composition of a country's exports in terms of both the types of goods it exports and the markets to which it exports.[15] Applying this analytical approach basically entails decomposing the change in German exports between any two periods into four effects: the effect from the expansion of overall trade by competitor countries (the global market growth effect); the effect from Germany's exporting goods for which demand is growing at a different pace than the overall average for competitor countries (the commodity composition effect); the effect from Germany's exporting to markets for which demand is growing at a different pace than the overall average for competitor countries (the market distribution effect); and a "competitiveness" residual.

More formally, the change in German exports (ΔX) between any two periods can be written as

$$\Delta X =$$

$$\sum_i r\, X_i \tag{1}$$

$$+ \sum_i r_i\, X_i - \sum_i r\, X_i \tag{2}$$

$$+ \sum_i \sum_j r_{ij}\, X_{ij} - \sum_i r_i\, X_i \tag{3}$$

$$+ \Delta X - \sum_i \sum_j r_{ij}\, X_{ij} \tag{4}$$

where r = the proportional change in the overall exports of competitor countries;
r_i = the proportional change in competitors' exports of good i;
r_{ij} = the proportional change in competitors' exports of good i in market j;
X_i = German exports of good i;
X_{ij} = German exports of good i to market j.

---

[15]More discussion of constant market share analysis is contained in Leamer and Stern (1970, pp. 171–83) and Richardson (1971, pp. 227–39).

Table 2-1. Constant Market Share Decomposition of Export Growth[1]
(In percent)

	1984–90	1984–87	1987–88	1987–90	1991–92	Memorandum item, 1990–92
Proportion of change due to						
Market growth effect	71.4	51.8	156.4	118.1	89.5	116.3
Commodity composition effect	7.5	8.0	8.7	3.4	6.9	11.3
Market distribution effect	16.4	16.2	–9.3	8.2	–59.9	–58.6
Competitiveness effect	4.7	23.9	–55.7	–29.8	63.5	31.0
Total	100.0	100.0	100.0	100.0	100.0	100.0
Memorandum items						
Yearly average growth in exports (percent per year)	15.1	19.7	9.8	10.6	6.9	3.9
Yearly average growth in exports due to competitiveness effects (percent per year)	1.0	5.4	–5.5	–3.6	4.4	1.2

Source: IMF staff estimates.

[1]Data for Germany are on a unified basis starting in 1991. Thus, calculations are generally not made that use data from 1991 on, against data for 1990 or earlier as a base; the calculations for 1990–92 are an exception and only for reference.

Expression (1) of the decomposition is the "market growth effect"; expression (2) is the "commodity composition effect"; expression (3) is the "market distribution effect"; and expression (4) is the residual "competitiveness effect." Expressions (2) and (3) take into account whether German exports are concentrated in commodities and markets that can be considered to be slowly or rapidly expanding relative to the average for competitors.[16]

The competitor group—that is, the standard by which to judge export performance—is taken to be the Organization for Economic Cooperation and Development (OECD), excluding Germany.[17] This helps meet the large data requirements, as detailed data are available on the value of exports across ten broad product categories and across various country markets that are aggregated (OECD series-C foreign trade statistics);[18] the analysis considers 11 market groupings.[19] Similar data are also available for Germany alone. Thus, r, the r_is, and the r_{ij}s are derived from data on OECD exports (excluding Germany) by SITC category and by market.

The results of this exercise are reported in Table 2-1; they extend to 1992 but do not go further because of data limitations. Also, starting in 1991, the data encompass unified Germany. As a result, the data for that year and 1992 are not strictly comparable with earlier data, and, for this reason, such comparisons are generally not made; however, the table does include reference calculations that compare 1992 to 1990. Table 2-2 summarizes the results for those goods and markets that are responsible for most of the observed change in overall market shares.

Looking over the whole sweep from 1984 to 1990, a negative competitiveness effect might have

---

[16]Reversing the order of calculating effects (2) and (3) would give a different decomposition but not change the calculations of their combined effects.

[17]A considerable bias might have been introduced in the interpretation of the competitiveness residual if the German economy were growing at a significantly different rate than the OECD average. In fact, real growth in west Germany, and for the OECD overall, averaged about 2½ percent from 1980 to 1992.

[18]Although it would have been desirable to perform the analyses on volume data to try to control for valuation effects, such data are not available.

[19]The 11 market groupings are North America; Japan; Australia, New Zealand, and South Africa; the 12 European Union countries; the European Free Trade Area; Asia; Africa; Latin America and the Caribbean; the Middle East; the economies in transition; and others not classified elsewhere, or a residual market. The one-digit SITC classification is section 0 for food and live animals; section 1 for beverages and tobacco; section 2 for inedible crude materials, except fuels; section 3 for mineral fuels, lubricants, and related materials; section 4 for animal and vegetable oils, fats, and waxes; section 5 for chemicals and related products; section 6 for manufactured goods classified chiefly by material; section 7 for machinery and transport equipment; section 8 for miscellaneous manufactured articles; and section 9 for commodities and transactions not classified elsewhere.

been expected given the deterioration in competitiveness suggested by several of the indicators discussed earlier. In actual fact, the calculations yield a small but positive effect—that is, German exports increased by a somewhat greater amount than would have been expected had they grown by the same proportion as competitors' exports in each good and each market (expression (4) in the decomposition). It can be seen from Table 2-1 that about 5 percent of the increase in exports over the entire period was attributable to competitiveness effects, which resulted in an annual average boost to export growth of 1 percent. Table 2-2 indicates that machinery and transportation equipment, which in 1990 accounted for about one half of Germany's exports, was the sector driving the positive competitiveness calculations, particularly with regard to exports to Japan, North America, and Asia; the competitiveness effect was negative for exports to other European countries. The category of manufactured goods (classified chiefly by material) was also important, with the calculated gains in this sector not concentrated in particular markets.

It is tempting to conclude that exporters were able to hold on to, and even increase, market share, though at some cost to profit margins. It is also plausible, given the results, that some of the nonquantifiable elements of competitiveness had a significant positive impact on exports, offsetting (or even resulting in) real exchange rate appreciation. Another explanation is that German exports are relatively price-inelastic, income-elastic goods.[20]

It is worth emphasizing that the commodity composition and market distribution effects were also positive and larger than the competitiveness residual. This was the case over the 1984–90 period and also in the two subperiods of 1984–87 and 1987–90.[21] This result provides some evidence consistent with the notion that Germany has benefited from a "favorable" composition of exports. Especially strong effects were calculated for machinery and transportation equipment, with strong effects also calculated for other categories of manufacturing; the European market figured prominently.

The gains from a positive competitiveness effect over the 1984–90 period did not take place in a steady fashion, as demonstrated by separate calculations for the first and second halves of the period. The first half of the period, 1984–87, experienced

significant and broadly based positive competitiveness effects, attributable most strongly to the machinery and transportation equipment sector but also to two categories of manufactured goods and to the chemicals sector. The calculations indicate that competitiveness effects added about 5½ percent a year to export growth. By comparison, negative competitiveness effects retarded export growth in the second half of the period by some 3½ percent a year; these negative effects were concentrated mainly in the machinery and transportation equipment sector and were particularly strong in 1987–88. Negative competitiveness effects were also calculated for chemicals and manufactured goods (classified chiefly by sector), but their size was relatively small compared with the positive gains recorded in the first half of the period.

Because the calculations can be sensitive to the choice of base year, different combinations of base and comparator years were tried within the 1984–90 period, but the results did not change in a substantive way. Germany's share in world trade peaked at the beginning of the 1980s. Calculations using 1980 as a base—which is also a year that precedes the U.S. dollar's sharp upward move—show positive competitiveness effects for the periods 1980–87 and 1980–90.

Although the effects of an appreciating real exchange rate operate only with a lag,[22] it is striking that the calculations for more recent periods, such as 1991–92, again show positive competitiveness effects, concentrated once more around the machinery and transportation equipment sector. Interestingly, the market distribution effect was substantially negative, which reflects Germany's having exported goods to particular markets for which demand was comparatively weak. As shown in Table 2-2, this was especially the case because of a range of exports (machinery and transportation equipment, manufactured goods, chemicals, and food) to the economies in transition.

On balance, a competitiveness problem has not been particularly evident in the export flows, despite the deterioration in competitiveness suggested by several conventional cost indicators.

Sectoral Pressures on Profits

Although not a sustainable strategy in the long run, exporters may have tried to defend their market share by "pricing to market" and squeezing profits in

---

[20]The elasticities estimated by the Deutsche Bundesbank (1994b) for various measures of the real exchange rate are all (in absolute value) at 0.3 or lower in the short run and below 0.5 in the long run. Golub (1994) finds comparatively little responsiveness of German exports to changes in relative unit labor costs. These two studies do not report income elasticities.

[21]The combined effect for the 1987–88 period was virtually zero.

[22]Estimates from MULTIMOD, the IMF's multicountry macroeconometric model, would suggest that most of the effects take place in one year. But even longer lags, say up to three years, would fail to explain the positive competitiveness residuals that the calculations suggest for the 1991–92 period.

Table 2-2. Main Forces Behind Decomposition of Export Growth
(*In U.S. dollars*)

	1984–90	1984–87	1987–88	1987–90	1991–92
Commodity composition effect	Total = 17.0 of which Mach & trans = 14.5 Misc manu = 7.6 Min fuels = –4.9 Food = –2.2 Crude mat = –1.6	Total = 9.8 of which Mach & trans = 7.9 Misc manu = 4.1 Chemicals = 2.1 Min fuels = –3.3 Food = –1.1	Total = 2.5	Total = 3.5 of which Mach & trans = 1.2 Misc manu = 2.2 Chemicals = –1.7 Min fuels = –1.1	Total = 1.9 of which Mach & trans = 1.5 Misc manu = 1.3 Chemicals = 1.5 Manu goods = –2.0
Market distribution effect	Total = 37.2 of which EEC (Mach & trans) = 33.3 EEC (Manu goods) = 10.2 EEC (Chemicals) = 3.6 EEC (Misc manu) = 3.4 NAm (Mach & trans) = –5.5 ME (Mach & trans) = –5.3	Total = 19.9 of which EEC (Mach & trans) = 15.0 EEC (Manu goods) = 5.1 EFTA (Mach & trans) = 4.1 EEC (Misc manu) = 2.0 EEC (Chemicals) = 2.1 EEC (Food) = 1.9 ME (Mach & trans) = –3.1 AFR (Mach & trans) = –1.6 NAm (Mach & trans) = –1.5 ANSA (Mach & trans) = –1.0	Total = –2.7	Total = 8.5 of which EEC (Mach & trans) = 12.2 Japan (Mach & trans) = 1.9 Asia (Mach & trans) = 1.2 NAm.(Mach & trans) = –4.7 EFTA (Mach & trans) = –2.3 EEC (Manu goods) = 3.1 Transition economies (Manu goods) = –1.7	Total = –16.6 of which Transition economies Mach & trans = –6.1 Manu goods = –2.2 Misc manu = –1.0 Chemicals = –1.7 Food = –1.6 EEC (Mach & trans) = –3.4 EFTA (Mach & trans) = –2.1
Competitiveness effect	Total = 10.6 of which Mach & trans = 8.6 (Japan) = (3.6) (NAm) = (2.6) (Asia) = (3.1) (EFTA) = (2.3) (Res) = (1.1) (EEC) = (–5.6) Manu goods = 4.2	Total = 29.3 of which Mach & trans = 17.6 (NAm) = (6.3) (EEC) = (3.6) (EFTA) = (2.4) (Asia) = (2.0) (Japan) = (1.6) Manu goods = 4.9 Misc.manu = 3.5 Chemicals = 2.8	Total = –16.1 of which Mach & trans = –11.8 (NAm) = (–4.8) (EEC) = (–3.2) (EFTA) = (–1.1) (Asia) = (–1.0) (Res) = (–1.0) NIE = –4.0	Total = –31.0 of which Mach & trans = –17.0 (EEC) = (–11.4) (NAm) = (–5.2) NIE = –7.2 (EEC) = (–2.8) (EFTA) = (–1.7) Chemicals = –3.0 (EEC) = (–1.7) Manu goods = –2.4 (EEC) = (–3.1)	Total = 17.6 of which Mach & trans = 12.0 (EEC) = (5.7) (EFTA) = (1.2) (ME) = (1.1) (Res) = (4.9) Transition economies = (–1.0) Manu goods = 2.7 Misc goods = 1.4

Source: IMF staff estimates.
Food = food and live animals;
Crude mat = crude materials, inedible, except fuels;
Min fuels = mineral fuels, lubricants, and related materials;
Chemicals = chemicals and related products;
Manu goods = manufactured goods classified chiefly by material;
Mach & trans = machinery and transport equipment;
Misc manu = miscellaneous manufactured articles;
Res = residual market;
ME = Middle East;
AFR = Africa;
NAm = North America;
ANSA = Australia, New Zealand, and South Africa;
NIE = goods not included elsewhere;
EEC = European Economic Community;
EFTA = European Free Trade Area.

the short run. Empirical work by Knetter (1989) provides supporting evidence of this kind of behavior. He finds that for a selected group of ten products across several market destinations that German export prices denominated in deutsche mark are sensitive to exchange rate changes and that adjustments in these prices have tended to stabilize the local-currency prices in the destination market. Amid the appreciation of the deutsche mark, this would imply a squeeze on profit margins. Unfortunately, because of data problems, it is difficult to garner other direct, and more general, evidence on the extent to which profits may have been squeezed in firms—or the various sectors that produce tradable goods—as a result of their export activities or their efforts to compete with imported goods. The sectoral data that are available encompass both domestic and foreign sales and therefore need to be interpreted with great caution; also, many difficulties are encountered in trying to discern which sectors faced import competition most intensively, by constructing, say, import penetration ratios. That being said, the available data tend to lend only limited support to the notion that profits in the tradable goods sector were squeezed in 1991 in some subsectors of manufacturing, but no clear pattern emerges in earlier years.[23] These data are reported in Table 2-3.[24]

Prospects for Export Growth

Judgments about external competitiveness can be based not only on past performance but also on the prospects for international trade. In addition to a favorable export performance in 1994, particularly in some regional markets, concerns over external competitiveness have also been mitigated by recent labor market adjustments to competitive pressures.[25] The Bundesbank has noted that the efforts of German producers to export have been assisted by accelerated cost-cutting measures that were widely introduced in industry in the light of sluggish sales trends and that also improved international competitive-

ness.[26] Indeed, moderate wage growth, along with productivity gains (reflecting labor shedding), contributed to unit labor costs that actually declined in 1994. Moreover, the ongoing restructuring of the business sector should also be helped by the increased flexibility in the hiring and usage of labor inputs, which in turn contributes to improving the financial position and external competitiveness of enterprises.[27]

It is also noteworthy that the recent deterioration in several indicators of external competitiveness has not prevented a strong pickup in export orders. Relevant data on these orders are shown in Chart 2-5, along with survey data on export expectations by enterprises and actual export performance. Following the upward trend in 1993, manufacturing export orders in 1994 were 14 percent higher than a year earlier. Survey data have also been very positive on potential export growth. In view of these indicators and their past relationship with actual export performance, it seems reasonable to expect that exports will perform well in 1995.

Nevertheless, the export outlook for later years remains more uncertain. First, other European industrial countries are likely to have experienced wage moderation and productivity-enhancing restructuring in their tradables sectors; therefore, the ultimate effect of recent adjustments in Germany on Germany's external competitiveness is not yet clear. Second, recent indicators of stronger export performance may be related to the weak domestic demand that firms experienced in Germany. In this light, there is a risk that a pickup in domestic demand might dampen future export performance by reducing incentives for firms to penetrate new markets. Furthermore, although it may be reasonable to expect subdued wage growth in the period immediately ahead when Germany would still be emerging from recession, it is unlikely that real wage increases could be held below productivity growth in the medium term, particularly for those categories in which labor skills are in short supply. In the absence of greater wage differentiation with respect to skill levels, pressures on wages overall could develop that would adversely affect competitiveness in international markets.

Concluding Remarks

The analysis in this paper has shown the differing pictures of Germany's external competitiveness painted by the various indicators examined. A num-

---

[23]To be clear, this analysis focuses only on profits in Germany whereas the earlier discussion is in terms of German profits relative to competitor countries. It would appear from the data in Table 2-3 that the apparent decline in Germany's relative profit margins up to 1990 did not reflect extensive pressure on absolute profits margins at home.

[24]While detailed data are available only through 1991, Deutsche Bundesbank (1993) reports a loss of profitability in 1992.

[25]German exporters have recently recorded rapid growth in their trade with developing countries, particularly in Latin America and Asia. It appears that Germany has gained a stronger foothold in Asia and is increasing its export marketing efforts there, helped by improved competitiveness against Japanese producers because of the strength of the Japanese yen.

[26]Deutsche Bundesbank (1994a, p. 66).

[27]The 1994 wage round, in addition to producing settlements typically in the 0–2 percent range, included agreements to increase the flexibility of labor utilization.

Table 2-3. Profit Margins
(In percent)

Sector	1985	1986	1987	1988	1989	1990	1991	1992
				(After-tax profits)[1]				
All enterprises	1.9	2.1	2.1	2.2	2.1	2.2	2.0	1.5
Manufacturing sector	2.3	2.5	2.3	2.6	2.4	2.5	2.1	...
Of which								
Chemical industry	3.1	3.3	3.6	4.1	3.9	3.4	3.1	...
Manufacture of plastic products	2.7	3.1	2.9	2.7	2.6	2.6	2.6	...
Quarrying, extracting, and working up of stones and earth	1.9	3.7	3.6	4.0	4.5	4.3	4.8	...
Iron and steel industry	2.2	1.7	0.5	2.0	2.3	2.2	1.6	...
Nonferrous metal industry	1.2	1.3	1.5	2.3	1.5	1.7	1.2	...
Manufacture of structural metal products	1.9	2.3	2.2	2.3	2.9	3.8	3.0	...
Mechanical engineering	3.0	2.8	2.1	2.7	2.7	2.6	1.5	...
Manufacture of road vehicles	1.7	2.1	2.4	2.3	2.1	1.9	1.4	...
Electrical engineering	3.0	3.1	2.7	2.4	2.1	2.5	2.3	...
Manufacture of tools and finished metal goods	3.5	3.5	3.3	3.9	3.3	3.6	3.2	...
Woodworking	1.2	1.9	1.9	1.8	1.5	2.2	1.5	...
Manufacture of wood products	1.3	1.9	2.6	3.1	2.7	2.9	2.7	...
Processing paper and board	3.3	4.0	3.1	2.6	3.2	3.4	2.4	...
Textile industry	2.2	2.2	2.5	2.5	2.2	2.3	2.0	...
Clothing industry	2.5	2.7	2.9	2.6	2.1	2.2	2.6	...
Food and drink industry	1.3	1.7	2.1	2.1	1.5	2.6	2.2	...
				(Profits before income taxes)[1]				
All enterprises			3.3	3.5	3.4	3.5	3.2	2.5
Manufacturing sector			4.0	4.4	4.3	4.3	3.6	...
Of which								
Chemical industry			7.1	8.4	7.7	6.6	5.5	...
Manufacture of plastic products			4.3	4.3	4.1	4.1	4.2	...
Quarrying, extracting, and working up of stones and earth			5.5	6.2	6.8	6.6	6.9	...
Iron and steel industry			1.3	3.3	4.2	4.0	2.8	...
Nonferrous metal industry			2.5	3.6	3.1	3.2	2.0	...
Manufacture of structural metal products			3.4	3.5	4.3	5.4	4.8	...
Mechanical engineering			3.7	4.2	4.6	4.3	3.1	...
Manufacture of road vehicles			4.6	4.6	4.8	4.2	3.1	...
Electrical engineering			4.6	4.4	4.1	4.2	4.0	...
Manufacture of tools and finished metal goods			4.7	5.4	4.7	5.1	4.7	...
Woodworking			2.4	2.4	2.3	3.1	2.2	...
Manufacture of wood products			3.4	4.0	3.7	3.9	3.8	...
Processing paper and board			4.4	4.0	4.2	4.8	3.8	...
Textile industry			3.9	3.7	3.5	3.4	3.1	...
Clothing industry			4.1	3.8	3.2	3.3	3.8	...
Food and drink industry			2.9	3.0	2.3	3.6	3.1	...

Source: Deutsche Bundesbank.
[1] As a percent of turnover.

ber of them have shown a deterioration in Germany's external competitiveness, some by sizable margins, but it also appears likely that the standard measures based on the manufacturing sector alone have over-stated the weakness of Germany's external competitiveness position. In this regard, the analysis of broader-based real exchange rate indices, and the internal real exchange rate, supports this conclusion.

Chart 2-5. Export Indicators
(March 1990 = 100)

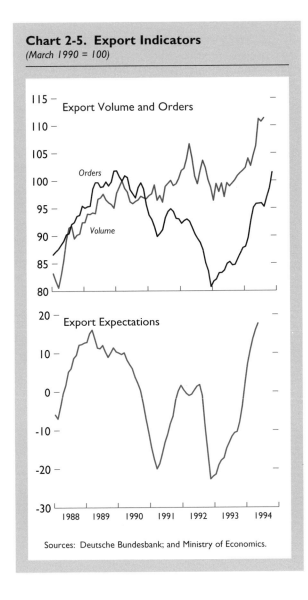

Sources: Deutsche Bundesbank; and Ministry of Economics.

tors of a worsened competitiveness position.[28] Looking to later years, however, there was good cause for optimism that economic recovery would not be thwarted by inadequate competitiveness and poor export performance. Quite the contrary, recent evidence on sustained growth in export orders and expectations through 1993 and into 1994, as well as actual export performance, are consistent with a solid rebound in exports. Significant adjustments have been and are taking place in labor markets, while enterprise restructuring continues, all of which are enhancing external competitiveness and export prospects. Sustaining a strong export performance into 1995 and later years will clearly be helped by a continuation of such restructuring and of labor market reforms and adjustments.

References

Adams, Gwyn, Lewis Alexander, and Joseph Gagnon, "German Unification and the European Monetary System: A Quantitative Analysis," International Finance Discussion Paper No. 421 (Washington: Board of Governors of the Federal Reserve System, January 1992).

De Gregorio, José, Alberto Giovannini, and Holger C. Wolf, "International Evidence on Tradables and Nontradables Inflation," IMF Working Paper No. 94/33 (Washington: International Monetary Fund, March 1994; to be published in the *European Economic Review*).

Deutsche Bundesbank (1994a), "Foreign Trade and Payments," *Monthly Report*, Vol. 46, No. 2 (February 1994).

———— (1994b), "Real Exchange Rates as an Indicator of International Competitiveness," *Monthly Report*, Vol. 46, No. 5 (May 1994).

————, "West German Enterprises' Profitability and Financing in 1992," *Monthly Report*, Vol. 45, No. 11 (November 1993).

Golub, Stephen S., "Comparative Advantage, Exchange Rates, and G-7 Sectoral Trade Balances," IMF Working Paper No. 94/5 (Washington: International Monetary Fund, January 1994).

Knetter, Michael M., "Price Discrimination by U.S. and German Exporters," *American Economic Review*, Vol. 79, No. 1 (March 1989), pp. 198–210.

Krugman, Paul (1994a), "Competitiveness: A Dangerous Obsession," *Foreign Affairs*, Vol. 73, No. 2 (March/April 1994), pp. 28–44.

———— (1994b), "Home Truths," *European Economic Perspectives*, Centre for Economic Policy Research, No. 3 (February 1994).

————, "Myths and Realities of U.S. Competitiveness," *Science*, Vol. 254 (November 1991), pp. 811–15.

Moreover, the results of constant market share analysis are revealing and actually suggest that a competitiveness problem has not been particularly evident in the actual performance of German exports. These results are particularly significant for the period up to 1990, insofar as an absolute squeeze on profits at home was not readily apparent. They also suggest the need to take into account product mix, quality factors, and market orientation in evaluating the international competitiveness of individual countries.

Developments in the more recent past have raised understandable concerns over Germany's competitiveness position. Notwithstanding the positive competitiveness effects calculated from the constant market share analysis for 1991–92, actual export performance, especially during the first half of 1993, worsened significantly on the heels of other indica-

---

[28]Export data for 1993 are subject to revision as the changeover to a new system of recording trade among European Union countries may have resulted in an underestimation of German exports to these countries.

Leamer, Edward E., and Robert M. Stern, *Quantitative International Economics* (Boston: Allyn and Bacon, Inc., 1970).

Lipschitz, Leslie, and Donogh McDonald, "Real Exchange Rates and Competitiveness: A Clarification of Concepts, and Some Measurements for Europe," IMF Working Paper No. 91/25 (Washington: International Monetary Fund, March 1991).

Marsh, Ian W., and Stephen P. Tokarick, "Competitiveness Indicators: A Theoretical and Empirical Assessment," IMF Working Paper No. 94/29 (Washington: International Monetary Fund, March 1994).

Masson, Paul R., and Guy Meredith, "Domestic and International Macroeconomic Consequences of German Unification," in *German Unification: Economic Issues*, IMF Occasional Paper No. 75 (Washington: International Monetary Fund, 1990).

Richardson, J. David, "Constant Market Shares Analysis of Export Growth," *Journal of International Economics*, Vol. 1 (1971).

Turner, Philip, and Jozef Van't dack, "Measuring International Price and Cost Competitiveness," BIS Economic Paper No. 39 (Washington: Bank for International Settlements, November 1993).

Wickham, Peter, "A Cautionary Note on the Use of Exchange Rate Indicators," IMF Paper on Policy Analysis and Assessment No. 93/5 (Washington: International Monetary Fund, March 1993).

III   Unemployment, Wages, and the Wage Structure

Tessa van der Willigen

Unemployment is perhaps the most pressing economic problem in Germany. Measured unemployment reached a postwar high of about 4 million people in early 1994, or about 10 percent of the labor force. This figure does not include about 1 million people who were kept off the unemployment rolls through special labor market programs in east Germany (job creation schemes, training programs, and early retirements). Unemployment and, to a lesser extent, the hidden unemployment embodied in active labor market programs bring a huge social cost. Both also bring large economic costs—the loss of the productive potential of people who would rather be working and fiscal costs.

High unemployment in east Germany was largely inevitable, as an obsolete industrial structure adjusted to new patterns of competition and as previously hidden unemployment emerged into the open. But west German unemployment, too, has been high and persistent since the early 1980s, except for a brief period around the time of the unification boom (Chart 3-1). West German developments are worrisome in their own right but also because of what they augur for east Germany: with western labor market institutions extended to east Germany, will a similar rate of unemployment prevail there in the medium to long term, or, worse, to the extent that unemployment displays persistence, will the rate in east Germany be lastingly higher? Thus, although the most pressing part of the German unemployment problem is in east Germany, the west German experience holds important clues to eastern as well as western prospects, and it is on this that the present chapter concentrates.[1]

Labor Market Developments

Measurement Issues

The commonly reported unemployment rate in Germany consists of the ratio of unemployed job seekers to the civilian labor force; this is the rate used throughout this chapter, unless otherwise noted.[2] Unemployed job seekers are defined as those who register as such with the Federal Labor Office, are available to take up a job, and currently work fewer than 18 hours a week.

The OECD-standardized unemployment rate for Germany (which is calculated by the OECD from labor force surveys) is typically much lower than the one based on national definitions: in 1993, it averaged 5.8 percent, compared with 7.3 percent for the commonly quoted rate. The OECD definition differs from the national one in three principal respects. First, the labor force is taken to include the military; however, this accounts for only a few tenths of a percentage point of the difference between the two rates. Second, the OECD defines as unemployed only those who have actively looked for work in the past four weeks. Third, and probably most important, the OECD defines as unemployed only those who did not work at all in the week prior to the survey. In the latter two respects, the OECD definition has the advantage that it does not count as unemployed those who are voluntarily unemployed or voluntarily working part time; but, conversely, it also eliminates from the definition of unemployment those who have been discouraged from actively seeking work and those who are working a few hours a week while looking for full-time work.

West German Employment and Unemployment

Unemployment in west Germany has registered three sharp rises since 1960 (Chart 3-1), only the first of which was reversed. Most worrisome was the third, which happened in the early 1980s: the long, albeit somewhat subdued, economic expansion of 1983–89 hardly lowered unemployment, which hovered around 8 percent—not far below its recent

---

[1]A more detailed examination of east German developments and prospects can be found in Chapter VI.

[2]A second commonly reported rate uses only the dependent civilian labor force (excluding the self-employed); indeed this is the most frequently quoted rate for east Germany. This rate is not used in this chapter.

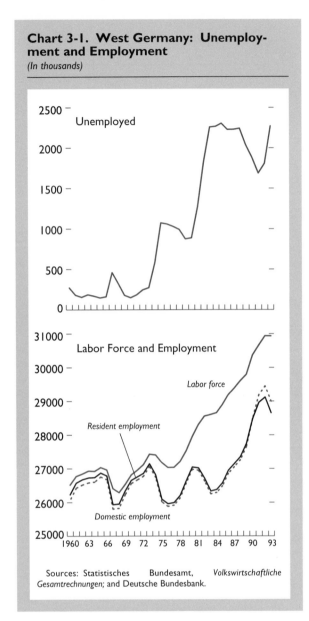

Chart 3-1. West Germany: Unemployment and Employment
(In thousands)

Sources: Statistisches Bundesamt, *Volkswirtschaftliche Gesamtrechnungen;* and Deutsche Bundesbank.

ple between 1980 and 1992. This trend almost entirely reflected a rise in the working-age population, owing first to the coming of age of the German baby boom (1980–88) and later to net immigration of more than half a million people a year (1988–92). Age-adjusted participation rates for the total population have remained rather stable: female participation rates have risen, but male rates have fallen, reflecting longer schooling and later entry into the job market. In addition to the growth of the (resident) labor force, a large net inflow of commuters from 1989 onward—including many from east Germany—dampened the rise in resident employment: the turnaround in the net number of commuters between 1989 and 1992 was close to half a million.

East German Employment and Unemployment

As in other planned economies, open unemployment was essentially unknown in the German Democratic Republic: enterprises simply employed the entire available labor force, whether it was productive or not. With the opening of the east German economy to market forces, this previously hidden unemployment emerged into the open in 1990. Employment was initially supported by liberal provisions for short-time work (subsidized by the Federal Labor Office), but they expired at end-1991, and, despite increases in the numbers involved in other active labor market programs, unemployment rose sharply (Chart 3-2). The number of unemployed, however, has risen only slightly further since the end of 1991, and employment appears to have stabilized.

Nature of Unemployment in West Germany

The OECD-standardized unemployment rate for west Germany is low compared with most other industrial countries. At 5.8 percent in 1993, it compares very favorably with an European Union (EU) average of 10.7 percent and ranks as the third lowest among the 17 industrial countries regularly monitored by the OECD (OECD, 1994a). Also on the positive side, the economy succeeded in creating a large number of jobs during the 1980s, and labor force growth is expected to be slower in the future, between –0.4 percent and 0.8 percent annually between 1995 and 2005, compared with an annual average of over 3 percent in the 1980s (OECD, 1994b). Nevertheless, west Germany has not been an exception to the Europeanwide trend of rising unemployment over the past three decades, nor is its level of unemployment—much less the level in east Ger-

level. The unification boom produced a short-lived reduction in unemployment, and with the 1992–93 recession unemployment rose again, to record levels.

The picture for employment, however, is very different. Paradoxically, employment grew little in the 1960s and 1970s (allowing for cyclical variations) and then rose rapidly during the 1980s and early 1990s, before turning down again since 1992 (Chart 3-1). A total of 2½ million jobs were created between the peak employment years 1980 and 1992.

At the same time, the labor force, which had hardly grown in the 1960s and 1970s (by less than 1½ million in 20 years), increased by 3 million peo-

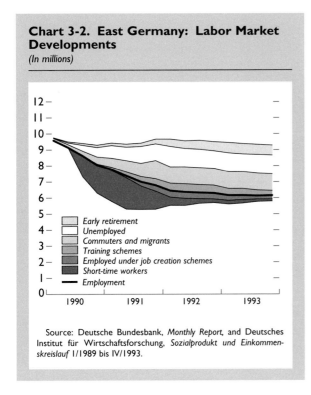

Chart 3-2. East Germany: Labor Market Developments
(In millions)

Source: Deutsche Bundesbank, *Monthly Report*, and Deutsches Institut für Wirtschaftsforschung, *Sozialprodukt und Einkommenskreislauf I/1989 bis IV/1993*.

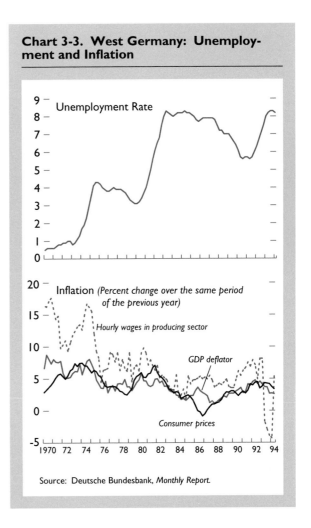

Chart 3-3. West Germany: Unemployment and Inflation

Source: Deutsche Bundesbank, *Monthly Report*.

many—considered acceptable. The puzzle of why the west German economy did not create sufficient jobs to accommodate the growing labor force in the 1980s casts an especially long shadow over prospects for east Germany.

Cyclical Unemployment Versus the NAIRU

In principle, unemployment can be decomposed into a cyclical and a "structural" component, with some interactions between the two, which are considered below. The structural component can be defined as that rate of unemployment that is consistent with stable wage-price inflation (the nonaccelerating inflation rate of unemployment, or NAIRU) and can be viewed as an "equilibrium" rate of unemployment. In other words, given a relation between unemployment and changes in inflation, only at the NAIRU is inflation stable and, other things being equal, does unemployment remain unchanged?[3] The significance of the distinction lies in the fact that, by definition, unemployment can be reduced—for in-

stance, by expansionary demand management policies—to the NAIRU, but not beyond it, without putting upward pressure on inflation.

There is little doubt that some of the current unemployment in west Germany is cyclical. The recession that began in mid-1992 was accompanied by a rise in the unemployment rate from 5.5–5.7 percent to a peak of 8.4 percent (May 1994). But the levels of unemployment observed around 1991 were exceptionally low. The persistence of unemployment rates well above 7 percent from the end of 1982 to the end of 1989, during seven years when GDP was growing at an average of 2½ percent a year, is prima facie evidence that a good deal of unemployment during the 1980s, at least, was not related to cyclical weakness. Indeed, all measures of inflation began to rise between 1987 and 1989, when unemployment was still above 7 percent, and the further declines in unemployment around the time of unification were accompanied by rising inflationary pressures (Chart 3-3). Casual observation would thus suggest

---

[3]The NAIRU concept is useful as long as there is a relation between unemployment and changes in inflation, regardless of its theoretical underpinnings—be they new classical, where deviations in unemployment from the equilibrium rate are associated with errors in expectations, or derived from models of monopolistic competition, where changes in inflation result from inconsistent claims by wage setters and price setters.

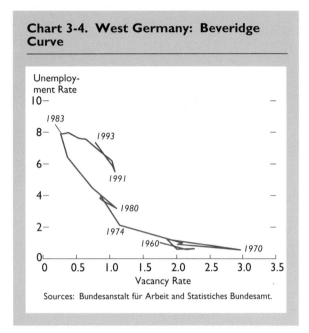

Chart 3-4. West Germany: Beveridge Curve

Sources: Bundesanstalt für Arbeit and Statistiches Bundesamt.

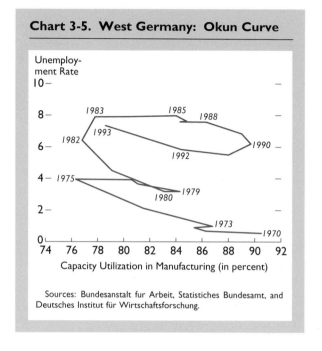

Chart 3-5. West Germany: Okun Curve

Sources: Bundesanstalt fur Arbeit, Statistiches Bundesamt, and Deutsches Institut für Wirtschaftsforschung.

rather strongly that by the end of the 1980s the west German NAIRU was not much below 7 percent. Indeed, a number of studies that have addressed this issue formally conclude that the NAIRU displayed a clear upward trend from 1970 onward—although there is little unanimity on its current level, with estimates in the studies ranging from 6 percent to 9 percent for the mid-1980s and early 1990s (Coe, 1985; Franz and König, 1986; Burda and Sachs, 1987; Elmeskov, 1993).

The Beveridge curve (Chart 3-4) also suggests that the NAIRU has risen. The curve relates the level of vacancies to the level of unemployment: since a cyclical increase in unemployment is normally accompanied by a fall in the vacancy rate, movements along the curve can be interpreted as cyclical movements, and shifts of the curve are indicative of a rise in structural unemployment. Chart 3-4 is strongly suggestive of a shift in the German Beveridge curve around 1983. Various studies have investigated this issue formally, concluding that the curve has indeed shifted (Budd, Levine, and Smith, 1987; Börsch-Supan, 1991; Franz, 1991).

A further indicator of cyclical unemployment, the Okun curve, relates the level of unemployment to measures of capacity utilization. To the extent that unemployment is accompanied by underutilization of capacity, it can fairly be called cyclical. Chart 3-5 shows the relation between unemployment and capacity utilization in manufacturing. The chart again strongly suggests a noncyclical rise in unemployment between the recovery periods 1975–79 and 1982–90. Studies by Schultze (1987) and Jaeger and

Parkinson (1990) formalize this conclusion by using the relation between cyclical unemployment and measures of capacity utilization to estimate the structural unemployment rate, which is found to be near 8 percent in the late 1980s.[4]

NAIRU: Friction, Market Failure, or Hysteresis

Thus, although it is difficult to quantify the exact extent of cyclical unemployment, it seems unlikely to account for more than a small portion (perhaps 1–2 percentage points) of west German unemployment of about 8¼ percent of the labor force in 1994. At the same time, simply knowing that the NAIRU is high is of little help from a policy perspective, since the concept is compatible with a variety of models of equilibrium unemployment. It is useful to distinguish among three different types of equilibrium unemployment, all of which may underlie the NAIRU.

In a market-clearing framework, equilibrium unemployment is *frictional*: the unemployed are engaged in a job search or are choosing leisure over work, and unemployment is essentially voluntary. The equilibrium level of unemployment will depend on factors influencing the effectiveness of the job search (such as skill or regional mismatch or the efficiency of intermediation) and on factors influenc-

---

[4]Schultze (1987) uses the OECD-standardized unemployment rate and on this (lower) basis estimates the NAIRU in 1983–87 at 6½ percent.

ing the choice between leisure and work (notably the level of unemployment benefits).

In a non-market-clearing framework, equilibrium unemployment can be involuntary, as long as some market failure stops wages from falling to market-clearing levels. For want of a better term, this chapter will refer to such unemployment as *market failure* unemployment. The most prominent contenders for the source of this market failure are efficiency wage theories and union power theories. In this framework, the equilibrium level of unemployment will depend in particular on the degree of unionization.

The difficulty with these concepts of equilibrium unemployment in west Germany is that none of these factors displayed the marked changes in the 1980s that would be required to explain the apparent rise in the NAIRU. Burda and Sachs (1987) conclude that frictional unemployment did not rise in the 1980s, because there was no increase in the generosity of benefits and only a slight increase in regional mismatch. Coe and Krueger (1990) allow for market failure unemployment as well as for frictional effects. They include in their estimation of equilibrium unemployment the age and sex composition of the labor force (the higher the proportion of the labor force that is prime age and male, the lower is frictional unemployment), the prevalence of apprenticeship programs (which again can be assumed to lower frictional unemployment), nonwage labor costs (which raise equilibrium unemployment if wages do not necessarily clear markets), the unionization rate, and unemployment insurance replacement ratios. They find that none of these factors explains the rise in unemployment in the 1980s and that, if the NAIRU were predicted on this basis alone, it would hover around 3½ percent from 1973 to 1988.

If the structural determinants of equilibrium unemployment (frictional and market failure) have not changed and yet the estimated NAIRU has risen with actual unemployment, a third, history-dependent type of equilibrium unemployment, *hysteretic* unemployment, must be allowed for. In the (unlikely) case of pure hysteresis, the NAIRU is simply the actual level of unemployment: any reduction in unemployment will put upward pressure on inflation. In the less extreme case of persistence, a unique NAIRU exists, but the speed of adjustment toward it may be very slow. In both cases, unemployment will appear to be a simple autoregressive process—a hypothesis which a number of studies on west Germany are unable to reject (Jaeger and Parkinson, 1990; Carruth and Schnabel, 1990). The presence of hysteresis is of particular importance to the assessment of the current level of unemployment: since hysteresis turns cyclical into structural unemploy-

ment, the economy may well emerge from the current recession with a NAIRU even higher than was estimated in the late 1980s.

Two main theories have been put forward to explain hysteretic unemployment. The human capital theory of hysteresis stresses that it is especially difficult for the long-term unemployed to reenter the labor market, both because their human capital has depreciated during the spell of unemployment and because employers view long-term unemployment as a signal of low productivity. By contrast, the insider-outsider theory of hysteresis stresses that the employed, as insiders, have power over wages—either because of institutional arrangements such as unions or because of transaction costs—and that an increase in the numbers of unemployed outsiders may do little to moderate insiders' wage claims.

Under both theories, the defining feature of hysteretic unemployment is a segmentation of the labor market between the "haves" and the "have-nots," so that long-term unemployment comes to constitute a rising share of total unemployment and that the average duration of an uncompleted spell of unemployment lengthens. The west German experience of the 1980s exemplifies these developments. Long-term unemployment (defined as more than one year) rose, peak to peak, from 15 percent of total unemployment in 1979 to 28 percent in 1991. The share of unemployment of more than two years' duration rose even more steeply, from 6 percent to 15 percent. The average duration of an uncompleted spell of unemployment rose from 7 months to 13½ months over the same period.

Segmentation of the labor market is also evident from the fact that rising proportions of the unemployed, and high proportions of the long-term unemployed, display one or more of the following characteristics: they are unskilled, they live in the north of Germany, or they are older.

The unskilled constitute a disproportionate share of the total number of unemployed. The unemployment rates for specific skill groups are shown in Table 3-1. Even though the reported unemployment rate for the unskilled is probably an underestimate (see footnote 2 to Table 3-1), it is much higher than that for the skilled. It is true that, as is commonly observed in times of robust growth, the unskilled unemployment rate dropped substantially during the 1990–91 boom; but the fact that inflationary pressures mounted even as the unskilled unemployment rate was still above 8 percent supports the view that the west German labor market is strongly dualistic. The share of the long-term unemployed among the unskilled is also disproportionately high. In 1988, 37 percent of the unskilled unemployed had been unemployed for more than a year, compared with 28 percent of the skilled unemployed.

Table 3-1. West Germany: Unemployment Rates by Skill Level[1]
(In percent)

	No qualifications[2]	Vocational training	Technical school	Technical college	University
1987	13.2	5.3	2.6	3.6	4.7
1989	12.1	4.7	2.4	3.4	4.3
1991	8.3	4.2	2.0	2.7	3.9
Memorandum item:					
Share in population in 1991	41.2	45.8	5.6	2.7	4.7

Source: Staff estimates based on *Bundesanstalt für Arbeit, Arbeitsstatistik,* and *Mikrozensus* (household survey) data as reported by the *Statistisches Bundesamt.*

[1]Skill levels are defined as follows: vocational training includes *betrieblicher Ausbildung* and *Berufsfachschule;* technical school is *Fachschule;* technical college is *Fachhochschule;* and university is *Hochschule/Universität.* "No qualification" is a residual and includes persons who did not report their qualifications.

[2]As the residual in unemployment, labor force, and population data, the group with no qualification is likely to be an overestimate; but the degree of overestimation is probably greater in the labor force data (because the question on qualifications is optional in the *Mikrozensus* survey) than in the unemployment data, which are taken from Labor Office records. The unemployment rate shown here is thus likely to be an underestimate.

In the same way as it is split by skill levels, the west German labor market also shows a pronounced north-south split. In 1991, unemployment rates across the Länder differed by almost 6 percentage points, with every one of the northern Länder registering a higher unemployment rate than any one of the southern Länder.[5] Equally striking is the evolution of these unemployment rates over time (Chart 3-6). All the southern unemployment rates peaked in 1983, but the northern unemployment rates peaked between 1985 and 1988. Clearly the recovery took much longer to have an impact in the north than in the south, and countrywide inflationary pressures began to mount even as nearly all northern unemployment rates were at or above 10 percent.

The wide dispersion of unemployment and the north-south divide existed in the late 1970s, with the variance of unemployment rates rising only a little between 1979 and 1991 (from 0.68 to 0.70). However, mismatch indices that take account of both unemployment and vacancy rates indicate a strengthening of the regional dimension of unemployment

over the 1980s.[6] Following Jackman and Roper (1987), two measures of mismatch can be calculated. With U and V referring to numbers of unemployed and vacancies, respectively, and the subscript i referring to regions,

$$M1 = 1/2 \sum \left| U_i/U - V_i/V \right|,$$

which can be interpreted as the share of the unemployed who would have to move to achieve regional balance, and

$$M2 = 1 - \sum (U_i/U)^{1/2} (V_i/V)^{1/2},$$

which can be viewed as the potential employment gain from such movement. Both measures show a sharp increase between 1979 and 1991—M1 from 13.8 to 22.6 and M2 from 2.0 to 4.3.

Regional mismatch is sometimes taken as evidence that unemployment is frictional, since it makes job searches less effective. This view, however, is easier to defend when pockets of high unemployment are geographically dispersed. Paqué (1989) points out that findings of increased mismatch at the Land level in west Germany are at variance with the results of studies of mismatch at a more disaggregated level (the 142 labor districts), which show much less of an increase. He concludes that unemployment has turned from a "spot" issue into a "cluster" issue, and the latter is more troublesome since both trickle-down effects and labor mo-

---

[5]For purposes of most regional comparisons in this chapter, the very smallest Länder are grouped with neighboring Länder, and Bavaria is divided into northern and southern Bavaria. Thus, the "northern" (really northwestern) Länder comprise Schleswig-Holstein (including Hamburg), Lower Saxony (including Bremen), North-Rhine-Westphalia, Rhineland-Palatinate (including Saarland), and Berlin-Brandenburg; the "southern" (really southeastern) Länder comprise Hessen, Baden-Württemberg, northern Bavaria, and southern Bavaria. The "central" states of Rhineland-Palatinate and Hessen are allocated according to structural features: Rhineland-Palatinate shares an important concentration on heavy industry with the northern states.

[6]Vacancy rates need to enter into measures of mismatch because there is no regional imbalance—merely differences in the efficiency of job search and intermediation—if high unemployment and vacancy rates coincide.

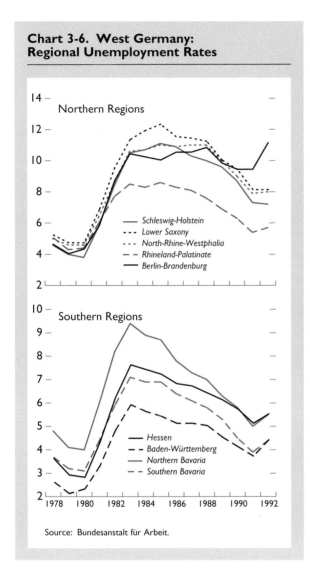

Chart 3-6. West Germany: Regional Unemployment Rates

Northern Regions
— Schleswig-Holstein
···· Lower Saxony
···· North-Rhine-Westphalia
– – Rhineland-Palatinate
— Berlin-Brandenburg

Southern Regions
— Hessen
– – Baden-Württemberg
— Northern Bavaria
– – Southern Bavaria

Source: Bundesanstalt für Arbeit.

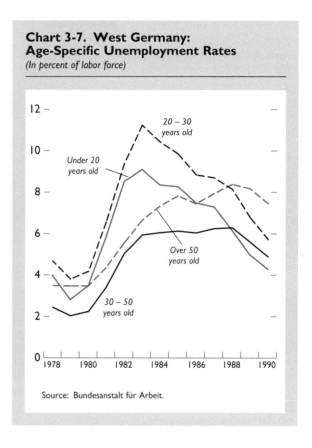

Chart 3-7. West Germany: Age-Specific Unemployment Rates
(In percent of labor force)

20 – 30 years old

Under 20 years old

Over 50 years old

30 – 50 years old

Source: Bundesanstalt für Arbeit.

bility are likely to be more limited between "clusters" than between "spots." The clear north-south split evident in Chart 3-6 suggests that clustering is a problem not only within Länder but also between groups of Länder. Overall, the picture that emerges is of a regional divide most probably brought about by structural change (the north being strongly dependent on heavy industry, such as mining, steel, and shipbuilding) and indicative not of increased length of job searches but of a marginalization of segments of the labor force.

A third dimension along which the west German labor market has become increasingly segmented is age. In contrast to many other countries where unemployment is concentrated among the young (a problem that is avoided in Germany thanks largely to the famous apprenticeship system), west German unemployment is increasingly concentrated among

older groups. As shown in Chart 3-7, the unemployment rate for those aged over 50 rose sharply between the cyclical peak of 1979 and the trough of 1983 and then continued to rise through 1989. From 3.5 percent in 1979, the unemployment rate for this group had reached 7.5 percent in 1990, well above the rates for other age groups.

In summary, there is evidence of an increasingly segmented labor market in west Germany, which has probably been a major factor behind the rise in structural unemployment. The unskilled, those in the north of Germany (most probably those with skills that have been devalued by structural change), and older groups of workers constitute marginal labor markets with far worse prospects than workers in the primary labor market. Whether these groups have become marginalized *as a result* of their unemployment, as the human capital theory of hysteresis would have it, is debatable. In the words of Paqué (1990), "the incidence of long-term unemployment is so strongly related to identifiable structural characteristics that it would be far-fetched to place much explanatory weight on processes of endogenous dequalification or demotivation." Instead, those who are marginalized in the labor market would appear to be those who started out with low human capital, at least as viewed from the perspective of a changing production structure. Even the high rate of unemployment of older workers may reflect the devaluation of skills in the course of structural change, as well as the need for worker flexibility and adaptability in the growing service sector. Either way, it would seem that groups of low-productivity workers have been priced out of the labor market. The next section describes the wage bargaining system and examines whether it might have contributed to labor market segmentation.

Wage Bargaining System

Key Institutional Features

Collective bargaining is enshrined in the German Constitution and in the wage contract law (*Tarifvertragsgesetz*) of 1949. According to the principle of *Tarifautonomie*, it takes place without the intervention of the Government. The partners to the negotiations are 19 national unions organized along sectoral lines and without occupational distinctions, 16 of which are members of the umbrella organization, the *Deutscher Gewerkschaftsbund* (DGB), and 1,000 employers' associations, which together form the *Bundesvereinigung Deutscher Arbeitgeberverbände* (BDA). On the employee side, only unions can enter into collective agreements; employers can negotiate as associations or individually.

The outcomes of the wage negotiations are a set of "tariff wages" by job grade (minimum basic wages) and provisions (typically in separate multiyear agreements called *Manteltarifverträge*) on working time, holidays, employment protection, training and retraining, and so forth. The wage contract law specifies that deviations from tariff wages are permitted only "in favor of the worker"—a provision known as the "favorability principle" (*Günstigkeitsprinzip*). Thus, although there are no further formal negotiations at the firm level, employers are free to set wages above tariff wages, and most employers actually pay wages some 10–20 percent above tariff wages. A second, informal round of wage negotiations does take place at the firm level between management and the legally mandated Workers' Councils (*Betriebsräte*); the Works Constitution Act (*Betriebsverfassungsgesetz*) of 1972 prohibits industrial action during this second round. However, in the great majority of cases wage structures are simply adjusted by the percentage increase in tariff wages. Profit sharing is little used in Germany. A few wage agreements provide for payment of bonuses at the employer's discretion, but in practice these bonuses have tended to become set amounts unrelated to profits.

Wage negotiations take place at the regional level, but national demands are publicized by the unions in advance of the wage round, and wage contracts are typically identical nationwide within a sector.[7] In addition, wage agreements in different sectors typically turn out to be very similar; in particular, the metalworking industry (represented on the workers' side by IG-Metall with its 3½ million members, amounting to one quarter of all union members in Germany), the public sector, and construction are the leading sectors, and the behavior of the other sectors has sometimes been characterized as "convoy behavior" (*Geleitzugverfahren*).

Union membership (the proportion of employees who are unionized) and union coverage (the proportion of firms covered by collective bargaining agreements) in Germany are quite different. Overall, about 40 percent of employees are union members—a proportion that, in contrast to many other countries, has remained rather stable since the late 1970s. But the applicability of the collective wage agreements is much wider than data on union membership might indicate. All employers who are members of an employers' federation are bound to pay at least the union-negotiated wage: they cannot hire union members below tariff wages, and morale considerations typically dictate that union and nonunion members be paid the same. Even if this were not the case, nonunion members can claim tariff wages through the courts on the basis of the "equal treatment" provisions of the labor law. It has been estimated that traditionally in west Germany's manufacturing and financial sectors no less than 80 percent of employers, employing 90 percent of workers in these sectors are members of employers' associations (Soltwedel, 1988).

Even if a firm and its workforce are agreed that wages should fall below tariff wages, perhaps to safeguard employment or the firm's very existence, the "favorability principle" has been interpreted by the courts to mean that this agreement can only be made as a formal exception to the collective agreement. Thus, unless the collective agreement explicitly states otherwise, the firm must ask its employers' federation to negotiate its individual case with the union. Soltwedel (1988) suggests that such requests meet with little sympathy because "the intramarginal members of the [employers'] cartel would prefer endangered firms to go bankrupt."

---

[7]Streeck (1988) suggests that wage negotiations are formally conducted at the regional level largely so that (costly) strikes can be limited to "pilot areas." To obtain uniform conditions across the country, the union relies on the incentives for the employers' association to eliminate wage-based competition and thus to make all its regional affiliates sign similar agreements.

In addition, even employers who are not members of employers' federations may become subject to the collective bargaining agreements as a result of "declarations of general validity" (*Allgemeinverbindlichkeitserklärungen*). According to the wage contract law, in a sector in which more than half the employees are employed by firms that are party to the collective agreements, either bargaining party may request that the Minister of Labor declare the collective agreement to be binding on all employers in the sector, regardless of whether they are members of an employers' association. The only—ill-defined—condition such a declaration must satisfy is that it be "in the public interest." Recently these declarations have been little used (about 2 percent of all contracts in 1993, estimated to cover a similar or marginally higher proportion of the workforce), and, when they have been, it has typically been for contracts relating to working conditions rather than to wages.

Aggregate Real Wages

The extent of the centralization of wage bargaining is generally thought to affect the degree of wage moderation, with important effects on overall employment (Calmfors and Driffill, 1988). The relation between centralization and average real wages is thought to be hump shaped: both decentralized and centralized systems may be compatible with wage moderation, while intermediate systems—industry-level bargaining, in particular—may be less so.[8]

The theoretical basis for this relation is that increasing union power at higher levels of centralization is offset by the fact that a number of externalities become internalized, as unions take into account the effect of their demands on other parts of the economy. Key among these externalities are price externalities (wage increases raise prices for other people), fiscal externalities (if wage increases give rise to unemployment, the corresponding unemployment benefits are partly funded by other people), unemployment externalities (higher unemployment makes it more difficult for other people to find jobs), and envy externalities (wage increases reduce other people's welfare to the extent that they care about relativities). In addition, centralization may improve coordination and prevent the excessive wage increases that can ensue under imperfect information when each union tries to prevent its own wage increase from falling short of the national average, so that each has an incentive to err on the side of excess (Bhaskar, 1990).

The German system, while an example of industry-level bargaining, appears to reap many of the benefits of centralization and is generally ranked just behind Austria and the Nordic countries in its degree of centralization. Two factors justify this view of the German system. First, it can be characterized as "pattern bargaining" (Flanagan, Soskice, and Ulmann, 1983), in which leading sectors (and, within sectors, leading regions) set the standard for wage increases throughout the economy. Pattern bargaining is by no means identical to centralization, because the leading sector may take only its own interests into account. But compared with pure industry-level bargaining, some externalities are internalized, since the interests of the leading sector are affected by the wage increases that it knows will follow elsewhere in the economy. Second, cooperation between employers and unions in the different sectors, institutionalized in Germany under the umbrellas of the DGB and the BDA, also helps to internalize externalities and overcome the informational problems that might lead each union to demand excessive wage increases.

Wage Relativities

Although centralization appears to be conducive to overall real wage moderation, it also reduces the ability of wages to respond to conditions in different parts of the labor market. The literature has recently paid considerable attention to wage dispersion, although it has not always distinguished clearly between dispersion across firms (including across groups of firms by sector or by region) and differentiation across categories of workers (including by skill level or age). This chapter will refer to the former as "wage dispersion" and the latter as "wage differentials."

There is evidence that the centralized systems that tend to produce real wage moderation also tend to produce low *wage dispersion across firms* (Freeman, 1988; Rowthorn, 1992), as might be expected since uniform wage contracts leave less scope for "tailoring" to the conditions of individual firms. Although the correlation between centralization and wage dispersion makes it difficult to separate the effects of each of these on employment, the same studies suggest a weak link between higher wage dispersion and higher employment across countries.

In a truly centralized system, low wage dispersion arises both because low-productivity firms pay relatively high wages and because high-productivity firms pay relatively low wages (both compared with the outcome under a decentralized system, at least in the short run). If these firms are thought of as constituting two separate labor markets, excess supply of labor will arise in the low-productivity labor market and excess demand for labor will arise in the high-productivity market. If labor can move freely be-

---

[8]Centralized systems are often also associated with low wage dispersion, which has detrimental effects on employment. These effects are discussed in the next section.

tween the two markets (for example, if the only difference between the two markets is the technology the firms use), the result for total employment is ambiguous: it may be higher or lower than with decentralized wage setting. However, if labor mobility between the two markets is limited (perhaps because the two markets require different skills or because they are geographically separated), total employment will be lower than if both markets cleared.

In an intertemporal setting, such wage equalization has a further effect, one that has formed the explicit basis for the solidaristic wage policies of unions in Nordic countries (see, for example, Flanagan, Soskice, and Ulmann, 1983) and that has been used to justify rapid convergence of east German wages to west German levels. The exclusion of low-productivity firms from the market and the high profits earned by high-productivity firms will strengthen incentives for productivity enhancements and structural change. But as Calmfors (1993) points out, even if the capital stock is younger, on average, with wage equalization, it may also be smaller: incentives to invest will be dampened by the fact that wages are foreseen to grow at the economywide rate of productivity growth, even though the productivity of a particular vintage of capital will remain unchanged. Overall, it is not clear that even the intertemporal effects of wage equalization among firms are by themselves beneficial.

Moreover, the German wage bargaining system does not generate true wage equalization because of the presence of wage drift at the firm level: firms are free to pay wages higher, but not lower, than those agreed centrally. Thus, when excess demand arises in the high-productivity labor market, wages there will rise, eliminating the already limited opportunities for labor to move to this market and thereby the outside chance that total employment might be higher than under flexible wages. The intertemporal benefits of wage equalization, too, will be muted in the presence of wage drift, since the high profits that high-productivity firms make under a policy of wage equalization will be eroded. Thus, on balance, there is considerable doubt as to the beneficial effects of wage equalization among firms even in fully centralized systems, and even more doubt about centralized systems with wage drift, such as the German one.

At the same time, it seems plausible—as suggested, for instance, by casual observation of the U.S. and European wage structures—that centralization will be accompanied by low *wage differentials across workers*. Such a result would not necessarily follow from the institutional setup (since a fully centralized system can still set widely different wages for different categories of workers) but from the

unions' objectives. There is much evidence that unions are averse to income inequality, perhaps because union members—and workers in general—are disportionately in the lower end of the productivity distribution (Freeman, 1980). Because of the limited or nonexistent mobility of workers between categories (such as those based on skill or age), the potential employment-increasing effects of wage equalization across firms do not arise in this case: squeezing wage differentials must have unambiguously negative effects on employment.

Wage Developments

The theoretical considerations outlined above suggest that the level of *real wages in aggregate* should be less of a concern in Germany than in true industry-level bargaining systems. Nonetheless, a number of studies in the 1980s (Artus, 1984; Burda and Sachs, 1987) concluded that unemployment in west Germany in the early to mid-1980s, in the aftermath of the oil shock, was at least partly traceable to excessively high labor costs, especially in manufacturing: actual wages were estimated to exceed warranted wages by up to 25 percent. However, this aggregate "wage gap" diagnosis has lost some of its appeal in the wake of subsequent wage moderation. Labor cost growth lagged productivity growth significantly from about 1984 onward (Chart 3-8)—despite the fact that the wedge between total labor costs and take-home pay rose from 78 percent of net wages in 1984 to 86 percent in 1993. While the endogeneity of productivity means that the development of unit labor costs can only be suggestive of a declining wage gap, Landmann and Jerger (1993) estimate, on the basis of trend rather than actual productivity growth, that the wage gap had disappeared by 1987–91.[9]

However, even if real wages are not excessively high in aggregate, wage dispersion or wage differentials—in the terminology of the previous section—may still be insufficient to allow full employment. The former would explain the concentration of unemployment in structurally similar regions (given less-than-perfect mobility of workers between regions or sectors), and the latter the concentration of unemployment among the low skilled. Because it is impossible to establish empirically how much wage differentiation is "adequate," an investigation of this proposition must rely on compar-

---

[9]The use of trend productivity growth circumvents the problems associated with the effect of wages on productivity through short-run fluctuations in employment but not the effect through capital accumulation. Indeed, Landmann and Jerger favor a capital shortage explanation of unemployment.

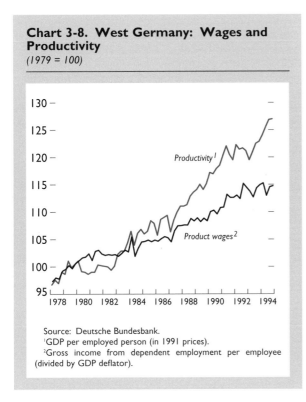

Chart 3-8. West Germany: Wages and Productivity
(1979 = 100)

Source: Deutsche Bundesbank.
[1]GDP per employed person (in 1991 prices).
[2]Gross income from dependent employment per employee (divided by GDP deflator).

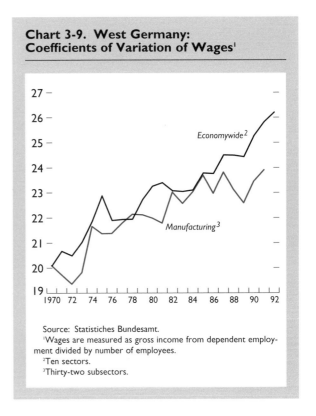

Chart 3-9. West Germany: Coefficients of Variation of Wages[1]

Source: Statistiches Bundesamt.
[1]Wages are measured as gross income from dependent employment divided by number of employees.
[2]Ten sectors.
[3]Thirty-two subsectors.

isons with other countries or with Germany itself in other periods, and the conclusions can only be suggestive.[10] The Appendix to this chapter gives a more detailed review of the relevant empirical studies for Germany.

Cross-country studies have found that west Germany has a moderate degree of *wage dispersion across sectors*, one that is much lower than that of the United States but generally higher than that of the Nordic countries. Although many authors (for example, Bell and Freeman, 1987) rightly urge caution in interpreting results for the United States as a benchmark, and although U.S. labor markets are by no means free of rigidities the argument in the previous section suggests that the United States, with its much more decentralized wage setting, should come closer to market-clearing wage dispersion than Germany does. These results suggest, therefore, that German wage dispersion may be insufficient.

During the 1980s, dispersion in west Germany rose across sectors (Chart 3-9), though much more weakly within manufacturing than economywide. Comparing changes in dispersion across countries in the 1980s, most studies find that wage dispersion rose more slowly in west Germany than in other countries, particularly the United States. To the extent that advanced economies were subjected to similar forces of structural change in the 1980s—technological change and increasing competition from developing countries in labor-intensive sectors—this comparison suggests that German wages reacted less flexibly to external shocks than did those of many other countries.

West German wage dispersion across regions fell between the 1979 and 1991 peaks of the economic cycle (Chart 3-10) despite the growing differences in regional labor market conditions. Indeed, the annual growth of wages between 1979 and 1991 varied by only 0.6 percentage point across the regions, with wages in the northern Länder rising by 4.1–4.6 percent a year and those in the southern Länder by 4.6–4.7 percent a year.[11] These observations are again suggestive of insufficient wage flexibility.

---

[10]A further complication is that the structure of earnings is sensitive to the economic cycle. Monthly earnings especially are more cyclically sensitive for the lower paid than for the higher paid. But recessions are also normally associated with a relative lowering of hourly earnings at the bottom of the scale, both because of slacker competition for labor and because low-skilled workers are more likely to be laid off in a recession. For these reasons, comparisons highlighted in this chapter are peak-to-peak (1979–91) wherever possible.

---

[11]All the Länder are considered separately in this comparison; the range quoted excludes Bremen, a northern city-state where wage growth reached 4.9 percent.

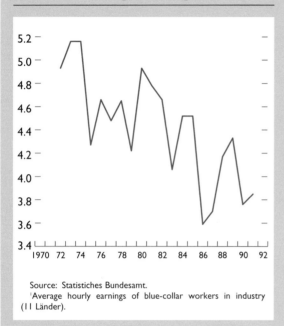

Chart 3-10. West Germany: Coefficients of Variation of Regional Wages[1]

Source: Statistiches Bundesamt.

[1]Average hourly earnings of blue-collar workers in industry (11 Länder).

country comparisons of wage differentials to the point of irrelevance. However, two main studies have examined trends in wage differentials in west Germany by focusing on the relations between the 90th, 50th, and 10th percentiles of the earnings distribution. OECD (1993) finds that earnings at the 90th percentile of the wage distribution rose slightly (1 percentage point) relative to median earnings between 1981 and 1990, but that earnings at the 10th percentile rose substantially (4 percentage points) relative to the median over the same period (Table 3-2). Abraham and Houseman (1993) also conclude that wage differentials in west Germany narrowed during the 1980s.

Narrowing wage differentials at the bottom of the pay scale appear to be related primarily to a reduction in education-skill differentials. Table 3-3 suggests that between 1979 and 1991, when most sub-sectors of manufacturing (22 out of 32) saw a widening of wage differentials between high-skilled and medium-skilled workers, the majority (23 out of 32) also saw a reduction in differentials between medium-skilled and low-skilled workers. Several studies that have estimated standard earnings functions on panel data also suggest some narrowing of education and training differentials in the second half of the 1980s, with the major change a decline in the premium for holding a vocational qualification (typically a completed apprenticeship).

The narrowing of wage differentials at the bottom of the scale is of particular concern in light of the high unemployment among unskilled workers. In-

The issue of wage differentials between workers is perhaps even more important in Germany, given the concentration of unemployment among the low skilled. Definitional problems complicate cross-

Table 3-2. West Germany: Ratios of Percentiles of the Earnings Distribution[1]

(Ratio)

	1979	1980	1981	1985	1986	1987	1988	1989	1990
Both sexes, GSOEP									
90/50	...	...	1.63	1.65	1.64	1.64	1.62	1.64	1.64
10/50	...	...	0.61	0.63	0.63	0.65	0.65	0.67	0.65
Men, social security									
90/50	1.47	1.47	1.47	...	...	...	...	...	...
10/50	0.67	0.67	0.68	...	...	...	...	...	...
Men, GSOEP									
90/50	...	...	1.63	1.66	1.66	1.63	1.65	1.65	1.65
10/50	...	...	0.68	0.70	0.70	0.71	0.71	0.72	0.71
Women, GSOEP									
90/50	...	...	1.56	1.58	1.62	1.58	1.58	1.59	1.58
10/50	...	...	0.59	0.63	0.64	0.65	0.67	0.66	0.66

Source: OECD (1993); GSOEP stands for German Socio-Economic Panel data.

[1]Earnings are gross monthly earnings plus benefits (calculated as one twelfth of 13th and 14th month pay, holiday allowances, and Christmas allowances) of full-time, full-year workers. Data are taken from social security records or from the GSOEP, Waves 1–8. 90/50 indicates the ratio of the 90th percentile to the median, 10/50 the ratio of the 10th percentile to the median.

Table 3-3. West Germany: Ratios of Earnings of Different Skill Groups in Manufacturing Industry[1]
(Ratios of hourly earnings)

Industry	High skill/ low skill		Low skill/ unskilled	
	1979	1991	1979	1991
Stones and clay	1.05	1.06	1.09	1.07
Iron and steel	1.06	1.09	1.06	1.06
Noniron metals	1.07	1.08	1.06	1.04
Mineral oil	1.16	1.19	1.12	1.23
Chemicals	1.10	1.12	1.19	1.20
Chemical fibres	1.00	1.02	1.11	1.03
Lumber	1.06	1.11	1.13	1.09
Pulp	1.08	1.08	1.07	1.09
Rubber	1.09	1.07	1.15	1.03
Steel implements	1.13	1.14	1.15	1.07
Machinery	1.12	1.13	1.09	1.07
Vehicles	1.11	1.10	1.11	1.12
Ships	1.19	1.21	1.11	1.13
Airplanes	1.22	1.22	1.13	1.12
Electrotechnical	1.14	1.14	1.04	1.04
Optics, watches, etc.	1.14	1.13	1.09	1.06
Metal finishing	1.10	1.11	1.10	1.09
Office machines	1.15	1.16	1.09	1.10
Ceramics	1.04	1.07	1.11	1.09
Glass	1.10	1.13	1.14	1.02
Wood products	1.12	1.10	1.12	1.09
Musical instruments	1.16	1.22	1.12	1.07
Paper	1.14	1.15	1.11	1.09
Printing	1.16	1.17	1.16	1.06
Synthetics	1.11	1.13	1.09	1.05
Leather manufacture	1.06	1.08	1.10	1.09
Leather products	1.12	1.11	1.18	1.09
Shoes	1.14	1.10	1.25	1.12
Textiles	1.10	1.10	1.10	1.09
Clothing	1.12	1.11	1.06	1.11
Food	1.10	1.12	1.09	1.11

Sources: *Statistisches Bundesamt*; and IMF staff estimates.

[1]Skill levels are the groupings defined in collective bargaining agreements: high skill, low skill, and unskilled—corresponding to *Leistungsgruppe* 1, 2, and 3 (master craftsman, completed apprenticeship, and unskilled), respectively.

dustrial countries have in recent years seen a shift in the demand for labor toward high-skilled workers, which has tended to widen wage differentials in most of them (see Katz and Murphy, 1992; Davis, 1992). Tellingly, the OECD (1993) study finds that, among 17 OECD countries examined, west Germany is the only one that shows a pronounced narrowing of wage differentials at the bottom of the distribution during the 1980s. Although the unique German system of vocational training may have played an important part in limiting the supply of the unskilled, high and persistent unemployment among the unskilled suggests that the narrowing of wage differentials was not purely an equilibrating response and that a lowering of wages at the bottom of the scale would benefit employment.

Key Labor Market Policies

The segmented nature of the labor market and the compression of wages at the lower end of the scale point to three policy areas that are likely to be of particular importance: the wage bargaining system and income support for the unemployed (which affect the lower part of the wage scale) and employment protection (which erects barriers between those with jobs and those without). This section reviews policies in these areas.

Recent and Potential Innovations in Collective Bargaining

Both the extension of west German labor market institutions to east Germany and the recession in west Germany have thrown into sharp focus the biases of the German collective bargaining system against low-productivity firms and workers. A measure of decentralization, within the framework of collective bargaining, was achieved in the 1980s with increased devolution of authority over industrial relations to the firm-level Works Councils (Streeck, 1988). But the debate over how to make the system more flexible, while preserving its essence, has now come to center stage. Although *Tarifautonomie* places the responsibility for the bargaining system squarely with the social partners, the Government retains a special responsibility to influence the debate both by rhetoric and example.

The rapid convergence of eastern wages to western levels is an extreme example of the way a centralized bargaining system tends to equalize wages between different firms. The convergence has been rationalized in part by the intertemporal arguments outlined above: higher wages in east Germany generate pressures for productivity growth and speed the "creative destruction" of the inefficient inherited production structure. However, the resulting very high levels of unemployment have brought a search for ways in which the wage bargaining system can accommodate less productive firms. Four main ways of doing this have emerged so far, although only two are consistent with the essential collective nature of the German system.

Perhaps the method that has attracted the most attention has been the introduction of "opt-out" clauses (*Härteklausel*) in wage contracts in east Germany. These clauses allow below-tariff wages to be paid if a firm and its workforce agree that there is a financial crisis. Such clauses allow the individual employer seeking an exemption to bypass the employers' federation. However, the regional-national union continues to be responsible for negotiating the exemption on behalf of the workforce. These clauses have been very little used, partly because the unions may be reluctant to allow the setting of low-wage precedents, especially when other avenues of survival (such as the seeking of subsidies or government guarantees) are still open to the firm. Placing the authority to negotiate exemptions at the level of the firm's Works Council might make such clauses more useful.

However, two other methods of paying below-tariff wages have emerged in east Germany. Employers have been pulling out of, or not joining, employers' federations: it is estimated that a quarter of employment in east Germany is in firms that are not members of employers' federations. In addition, even some firms that are members of employers' federations have been paying below-tariff wages, with the tacit agreement of their workforce, thus avoiding the need to seek union agreement on the use of an opt-out clause. Overall, it is estimated that 36 percent of east German firms pay below-tariff wages (as of early 1994). Of course, both these developments, if sustained, would represent a major departure from the collective bargaining system. But both the Government and the social partners have tolerated them as an appropriate response to a temporary and highly unusual situation in east Germany.

Finally, there have been moves in both west and east Germany toward greater flexibility at the firm level on points other than wages, in particular on working time. In the 1994 wage round, the metal-working and chemical sectors incorporated in their collective agreements a provision for working-hour "corridors." In the chemical industry, for instance, the uniform 37½-hour work week has been replaced by a "corridor" of 35–40 hours: workers who work less than 37½ hours receive commensurately less pay, and workers who put in more time receive standard, rather than overtime, pay for the additional hours. In addition, in a number of sectors, firms were given greater freedom to compensate overtime with additional free time rather than with extra pay. Both these developments provide firms with better opportunities to minimize their labor costs while continuing to pay tariff wages.[12] Further devolution of responsibility to the firm level for nonwage elements promises a better reconciliation of flexibility at the

firm level with the principle of collectively set wages.

Two further methods of injecting greater flexibility at the firm level within the confines of collective wage bargaining might be considered. The first is greater reliance on wage drift. Indeed, greater wage drift may well arise if the real wage moderation demonstrated in the 1994 wage round persists into the economic recovery. However, centralized unions will always have strong incentives to legitimize themselves by seeking substantial nominal wage increases. And these incentives become all the more problematic in the German environment of low inflation, where zero or negative nominal wage increases might well be called for if wage drift were to be substantial (Calmfors, 1993).

A second potential avenue for greater flexibility is profit sharing, which has been much discussed in Germany but little implemented. A base wage lower than current wages would both allow the survival of lower-productivity firms and reduce the marginal cost of labor more generally. However, as with recourse to wage drift, the benefits of profit sharing depend on unions moderating their wage demands: otherwise profit sharing becomes merely an additional claim on existing profits. Thus, although both wage drift and profit sharing appear to promise greater firm-level flexibility, this promise cannot be fulfilled without a public debate and a wholehearted commitment by the unions and their members to the notion of holding back tariff wages.

The search for ways to accommodate productivity differentials across firms within a collective bargaining framework has been accompanied by a similar search for ways to allow for greater productivity differences across workers. Structural change in east Germany, which has rapidly devalued human capital there, and the persistence of low-skilled unemployment in west Germany have added urgency to this search. Although some have argued that employing a willing worker who would otherwise be unemployed at a below-tariff wage is by definition a development "favorable to the worker," the "favorability principle" has been interpreted to mean that such arrangements are illegal unless explicitly provided for in the collective agreements. However, in 1994 for the first time, the collective agreement in the chemical industry incorporated a provision that allows new recruits to be paid (for one year) wages 5–7½ percent below tariff wages and 10 percent below tariff wages if they were recruited out of long-term unemployment. Whether this example will be followed elsewhere remains to be seen. Equally important would be a greater differentiation of tariff wage increases among skill levels. In both cases, the Government as employer could set potent precedents.

---

[12]Greater freedom to reduce working hours also reduces the fixed costs of employment and should help to reduce employers' reluctance to hire.

Income Support for the Unemployed

Regardless of the form of the wage bargaining system, the income level available to the unemployed plays an important role in determining net reservation wages and hence—once account is taken of the wedge between net wages and labor costs—in setting a lower bound on the productivity of those employed. The unemployed in Germany have recourse to three different kinds of assistance: unemployment benefit (*Arbeitslosengeld*), unemployment assistance (*Arbeitslosenhilfe*), and—together with others whose income is inadequate—social assistance (*Sozialhilfe*).

Unemployment insurance is compulsory for all employees except civil servants and soldiers. Unemployment benefit and unemployment assistance are paid to those who have contributed to the unemployment insurance scheme for at least one year out of the three years preceding unemployment, who have involuntarily lost their jobs, and who are seeking work. Those who voluntarily quit their jobs must wait 12 weeks before drawing benefits. Those who turn down one job offer that the Labor Office considers acceptable (*zumutbar*) have their benefits interrupted for up to 12 weeks, and those who turn down two such offers generally have their benefits terminated.

Both unemployment benefit and unemployment assistance are exempt from tax and are calculated as ratios of the worker's previous net earnings, excluding the typical 13th month wage. (Thus the replacement ratios typically quoted, and given below, are somewhat overstated: the official replacement ratio of 67 percent, for instance, translates into about 62 percent of total annual earnings.) The maximum net earnings to which the replacement ratios are applied are (for married persons with two children) about DM 5,070 a month in west Germany and DM 4,130 a month in east Germany, or close to twice average net earnings. The reference period for the calculation of the wage that serves as the base for unemployment benefits was three months until recently, but to combat collusion between employer and employee it was lengthened to six months, effective January 1994.

Unemployment benefit is generally payable for one year; for workers older than age 42, the period of eligibility rises with employment tenure and with age, up to a maximum of two years and eight months at age 54 or over. Until recently, unemployment benefit was payable at the rate of 68 percent of previous net earnings for a claimant with children and 63 percent for a claimant without children; from January 1994, these replacement ratios have been lowered to 67 percent and 60 percent, respectively. These ratios are not out of line with those in other OECD countries, though it might be noted that they are still above those that prevailed in Germany through the early 1970s (63 percent for a person with children).

After unemployment benefits have expired, unemployment assistance is currently available without time limit to those in need. It is also payable to most people in need who lost their jobs and were not entitled to unemployment benefit, but for them the period of eligibility, which until recently was also unlimited, was reduced to one year with effect from January 1994. Unemployment assistance was until recently payable at the rate of 58 percent of previous net earnings for a claimant with children and 56 percent for a claimant without children; from January 1994, these ratios were lowered to 57 percent and 53 percent, respectively. In principle, the wage to which these replacement ratios are applied is the potential wage rather than the actual previous wage, and, as the spell of unemployment lengthens and it becomes evident that no job with similar wages is available, the Labor Office is supposed to reduce the basis for the replacement ratio in line with their perception of the wage the unemployed person could potentially earn. Recipients must have no other means of support; if the recipient has other income or his or her spouse has income above DM 800 a month, the amount of unemployment assistance is reduced one for one.

The unlimited duration of unemployment assistance is a peculiarly generous feature of the unemployment insurance system. In 1989, the German replacement ratio for a single person in his or her third or subsequent year of unemployment was by far the highest in the OECD, exceeding the ratio in the next highest nation, the Netherlands, by 12 percentage points (OECD, 1991). Proposals to limit unemployment assistance to two years (first considered and then rejected in late 1993) were recently put forward as part of the draft 1995 budget. This measure would appear to hold considerable promise to reintegrate the long-term unemployed into the job market, both directly by raising incentives to work and indirectly by reducing insider power over wages through an increase in the search intensity of the unemployed.

Finally, social assistance (*Sozialhilfe*) is available for an unlimited period to anyone living in Germany whose income is inadequate to meet basic needs, although social assistance recipients who are able to work are required to register with the Labor Office and to accept appropriate job offers. The payments consist of cash allowances, contributions to housing and heating costs, and special one-off payments for necessary purchases. The amounts paid depend on family size and structure and on the ages of any children. Table 3-4 shows some typical amounts of social assistance and their relation to

Table 3-4. Social Assistance and Average Earnings[1]
(Deutsche mark per month)

	West Germany			East Germany		
	Average earnings	Social assistance	Ratio[2]	Average earnings	Social assistance	Ratio[2]
Single man	2,349	1,032	44	1,669	819	49
Single woman	1,985	1,032	52	1,287	819	64
Married, no children[3]	2,630	1,673	64	1,824	1,371	75
Married, one child[3]	2,782	2,159	78	2,019	1,764	87
Married, two children[3]	3,064	2,618	85	2,305	2,198	95
Married, three children[3]	3,426	3,066	89	2,668	2,652	99
Single person, one child	2,273	1,635	72	1,629	1,335	82
Single person, two children	2,571	2,122	83	1,876	1,730	92

Sources: Presse- und Informationsamt der Bundesregierung, *Sozialpolitische Umschau*, Nr. 11/1994 (January 1994); and IMF staff estimates.

[1]As of July 1992. Earnings are for blue-collar workers of *Leistungsgruppe* 3 and include child and rent allowances.

[2]Ratio of social assistance to average earnings (in percent).

[3]Assumes nonearning spouse.

average earned incomes of the lowest-paid group of blue-collar workers in west and east Germany for varying household structures. The difference is large only for childless people in west Germany and for single childless people in east Germany. For all others, the ratio of social assistance to average earnings is above 70 percent, and in east Germany the ratio is at 87 percent or above for people with two or more dependents. Social assistance is indexed not to prices but to wages, suggesting that the poverty line is defined in relative rather than absolute terms.

Decisions about the poverty line and about the respective importance of absolute and relative poverty are ones on which nations can have very different views. However, in making these decisions it is important to bear in mind their consequences for the labor market. Table 3-4 suggests that social assistance may provide very high replacement ratios for many low-skilled workers, as a result of which work may not be worthwhile. Conversely, since the level of social assistance is one factor affecting wage setting, Table 3-4 can be interpreted as confirming that social assistance effectively sets a floor on wages economywide. Using the figure in Table 3-4 for social assistance for a west German with two dependents (approximately DM 2,150 a month) as the reservation net wage, and adding social security contributions of about 50 percent of net wages, suggests that the effective minimum labor cost in Germany may be DM 3,200 (about US$2,000) a month, or over DM 20 (about US$13) an hour.[13] These minimum costs may exclude significant numbers of the unskilled or low skilled from (legal) employment and prevent some growth in sectors dependent on low-skilled labor, such as personal services.

Employment Protection

Segmentation of the labor market between the employed and the unemployed is often supported by employment protection for those with jobs. Such protection both increases insiders' power by raising transaction costs and reduces firms' willingness to hire by raising the fixed costs of employment. That there are serious obstacles to hiring in Germany is suggested both by employer surveys and by the fact that the German economy operates with considerable amounts of overtime even in periods of recession (Franz and König, 1986). Indeed, employment protection legislation in Germany is relatively severe and ill defined, and both the direct costs of dismissals and the uncertainties surrounding the courts' interpretation of the relevant legislation have probably contributed to a reluctance to hire: a hiring mistake, whether in assessing an individual recruit or

---

[13]Social security contributions add up to about 40 percent of gross wages, of which half is paid by the employee (out of gross wages) and half by the employer (in addition to gross wages). Thus, even abstracting from income tax, the wedge between net wages and total labor costs is about 50 percent. Income tax currently payable on gross wages up to the amount of social assistance is to be abolished by order of the Constitutional Court.

the appropriate level of employment overall, can be very costly.

Employment contracts in Germany are typically of indefinite duration. Dismissal protection applies to all permanent employees in firms with six or more workers (excluding apprentices), after a probationary period of six months. A notification period between four weeks and seven months is required, depending on the worker's seniority and age.

Individual dismissals have to be "fair," but criteria for fairness are only partially laid down in legislation. An employee may be dismissed for personal reasons, in particular, ineptitude; but in many cases personal reasons are not recognized as acceptable reasons for dismissal if the employer could fill the gap by other means, such as temporary reorganization or an increased workload for the remaining staff. Employees may be dismissed for redundancy only as a last resort—if the alternatives are "intolerable"—and the employer must use "social" criteria in choosing the redundant workers. It has been up to the courts to define both the "tolerable alternatives" to dismissals and the social criteria to be used in redundancies. In the latter case, criteria that have been adduced include period of employment, age, health, family responsibilities, spouse's income, and wealth. The burden of proof regarding the fairness of a dismissal rests with the employer, and employees who contest a dismissal must be allowed to continue in employment until the case is decided. If a dismissal is found to be unfair, the employee either remains in the job or is paid compensation equivalent to at least 12 months' pay (15–18 months' pay for older workers with longer tenure in the firm).

Overall, for strictness of protection, Grubb and Wells (1993) rank Germany fifth among 11 OECD countries, behind 4 southern European countries (Portugal, Spain, Italy, and Greece). But perhaps even more important than the rules laid down in the law is the discretion of the courts in the area of employment protection, which has created considerable uncertainty for employers. The Deregulation Commission recommended in 1991 that the definition of the social criteria used in selecting employees for dismissal should not be left to the courts, but this recommendation has not been implemented.

Collective dismissals at firms employing more than 20 employees are subject to even more stringent conditions. If more than five employees are to be dismissed within 30 days, the Labor Office must be notified of the dismissal and can delay it by up to two months. More important, under the Works Constitution Act, if more than 20 percent of the workforce or more than 60 employees are to be dismissed, management and the Works Council must agree on a "social plan" that stipulates compensation for those workers who are to lose their jobs. If the

parties cannot agree on a social plan, the case goes to binding arbitration. Since 1985, new firms have been exempt from the social plan requirement for the first four years of their existence. It has been estimated that payouts under social plans average four to six months of wages for a worker with average blue-collar industrial earnings. The Deregulation Commission had recommended that compensation under social plans be limited to damages directly related to the dismissal, but this proposal was not implemented.

The restrictions on dismissals also apply to workers on fixed-term contracts during the term of their contract, but the expiration of such a contract provides the employer an opportunity to reassess the employment decision. Fixed-term contracts are normally permitted in German law only under specified circumstances (such as for seasonal work in agriculture) and are not normally renewable. The Employment Promotion Act of 1985 made fixed-term contracts possible in any sector and under any circumstances, extended the maximum duration of fixed-term contracts from 6 months to 18 months (and 24 months for new small businesses), and made it possible to renew such contracts once. This law was due to expire in 1995, but its validity has recently been extended to the year 2000.

Conclusions

This chapter has suggested that only a small part of the German unemployment problem is cyclical in origin. More important, the west German labor market has become increasingly segmented, with a sharp division between the primary labor market and a marginal, high-unemployment, labor market consisting of the low skilled, those whose skills have been devalued by structural change (especially in the north), and older people. Economic recovery holds little hope for this secondary labor market, where a large amount of unemployment is likely to remain even when the primary labor market has tightened sufficiently to raise fears of rising inflation. The marginalization of people in the secondary labor market is worrisome in itself but also augurs ill for east Germany.

Both theoretical considerations and empirical studies of wage differentiation suggest that the German system of collective bargaining, which has served the country well in terms of overall wage moderation, has also resulted in wages that make it difficult for low-productivity firms and workers to participate in the labor market. The challenge now is to find, within the framework of centralized bargaining, ways in which relatively low-productivity firms can be assured better chances of survival (a challenge made especially pressing by the situation in east Germany) and ways in which wages at the bottom of the scale can react to the excess supply of low-productivity workers. Some progress has already been made in these respects, but much more is needed. Reform of unemployment insurance (especially the recently proposed limit on the duration of unemployment assistance), a reexamination of social assistance, and a reduction in the courts' discretion in the area of employment protection would support such efforts by reducing reservation wages and lowering barriers between the two labor markets.

Appendix: Wage Relativities in West Germany—A Review of Empirical Studies

An examination of whether wage relativities are "adequate" in Germany is complicated by the fact that there is no clear standard for what constitutes "adequate" differentiation. Two approaches to this problem have been taken in the literature, one based on cross-country studies and the other on time-series analysis. Because both require something of a leap of faith when using them as a benchmark for what constitutes "adequate" differentiation in a particular country or time, their results can only be suggestive.

Cross-country studies (Bell, 1986; Freeman, 1988; Rowthorn, 1992) have compared levels of wage dispersion across sectors and concluded that Germany has a moderate degree of it, one that is much lower than that of the United States but generally higher than that of the Nordic countries. Bellmann and Möller (1993) and Zweimüller and Barth (1994), in recent studies that control for human capital factors in an attempt to isolate sectoral effects, come to a similar conclusion comparing Germany with Sweden and the United States, and with Austria, Norway, and the United States.[14] To the—admittedly limited—extent that the United States, with its famously flexible labor markets, can be taken as a reference for what constitutes "sufficient" wage dispersion, these results suggest that German wage dispersion is insufficient.

Studies tracing changes over time have found that west German wage dispersion between sectors was stable or slightly increasing over the first half of the

---

[14]Human capital factors can bias aggregate comparisons of wage dispersion. For instance, a country where highly paid workers (say, more educated workers) are distributed more unevenly across sectors will show a lower degree of wage dispersion than one with a more even distribution across sectors, even if in each sector the two countries' pay scales are really identical. The most careful studies of dispersion, therefore, look not at average earnings in different industries but at the coefficients on industry dummies in standard earnings functions.

1980s (Bell, 1986; Gundlach, 1986; Freeman, 1988; Rowthorn, 1992; also see Chart 3-9 of this chapter). Bellmann and Möller (1993), in a study controlling for human capital factors, also conclude that wage dispersion across sectors rose in the 1980s.

However, west German wage dispersion, even though rising in the 1980s, may still not have risen enough from the point of view of employment creation. Again, cross-country studies have been adduced to explore how much of an increase is enough. Bell (1986), Freeman (1988), and Rowthorn (1992) all provide comparable estimates for the rise in wage dispersion in west Germany and the United States. They all find wage dispersion rising considerably less fast in west Germany than in the United States and other countries. Of course, using the United States as a benchmark here requires not only the assumption that its labor markets are more flexible but also the assumption that the changes in the structure of advanced economies in the 1980s were very similar. Because the main forces that induced structural change in these economies were probably similar—technological change and increasing competition from developing countries in labor-intensive sectors—this assumption may serve as a first approximation.

One further clue as to whether wages have been sufficiently flexible across firms comes from the dispersion of wages across regions. Gundlach (1986) found that within most sectors the dispersion of wages across regions narrowed between 1973 and 1985 (see Chart 3-10 of this chapter).

Definitional problems complicate cross-country comparisons of wage differentials to the point of irrelevance. However, both OECD (1993) and Abraham and Houseman (1993) have examined trends in west German wage differentials by focusing on the relations between the 90th, 50th, and 10th percentiles of the earnings distribution, using social security data and data from the German Socio-Economic Panel. Both studies find a significant narrowing of wage differentials, particularly at the bottom of the scale (see Table 3-2 of this chapter).

Both the Abraham and Houseman study and, to a lesser extent, the OECD study are open to the criticism that they do not take sufficient account of cyclical considerations as possible explanations for the changes in German wage differentials. The structure of earnings—especially the monthly earnings investigated in these studies—is not unrelated to the phase of the economic cycle. Monthly hours, and hence monthly earnings, of the low paid are more cyclically sensitive than those of the higher paid; for this reason alone, narrowing differentials of monthly earnings can be expected in a rising phase of the economic cycle. Also, recessions are normally associated with a relative lowering of earnings at the bottom of the scale, both because of slacker competition among firms for labor and because low-skilled workers are more likely to be laid off in a recession; a recovery would narrow wage differentials on this count as well.

While the 1983–90 period in Germany can be characterized as a long, slow recovery, two factors mitigate against a cyclical explanation of the narrowing of wage differentials at the bottom of the scale. First, the fragmentary data available for 1979–81, years when output is estimated to have been above potential, suggest that wage differentials narrowed during the 1980s even when comparing two cyclical peaks (around 1980 and around 1990). Second, despite a clear, though momentary, cyclical slowdown in 1987, the trend toward narrowing wage differentials continued unabated.

In many industrial countries, the 1980s saw increases in wage differentials by age. The evidence for this is mixed in west Germany. Based on aggregate data, Abraham and Houseman (1993) document a tendency for age-related earnings differentials to narrow slightly between the mid-1970s and 1988, with workers aged 15–19 gaining on those aged 20–29 throughout this period and workers aged 20–29 gaining on all older groups at least from 1983 onward. Similarly, they find a falling coefficient on age in their earnings functions between 1983 and 1988, but Bellmann and Möller (1993) find a rising coefficient on experience between 1979, 1984, and 1989.[15]

With age differentials playing a minor role at most, the narrowing of wage differentials at the bottom of the pay scale appears to be related primarily to a reduction in education-skill differentials (see Table 3-3 of this chapter). Abraham and Houseman (1993), using social security and GSOEP data classified by occupational qualification, conclude that there was a slight narrowing of the differentials between more and less educated workers from the mid-1970s to 1988. Both Abraham and Houseman (1993) and Bellmann and Möller (1993) also estimate standard earnings functions on panel data, using education and training dummies as well as age and other data. Both sets of results suggest some narrowing of education and training differentials in the second half of the 1980s, with the major change a decline in the premium for holding a vocational qualification (typically a completed apprenticeship).

Should such a narrowing of west German wage differentials be a source of concern from the point of view of employment, or was it an equilibrating response to changes in the supply and demand of different categories of workers? The study by Abraham and Houseman (1993) is the only one to address the issue of relative supply and demand for different categories of workers, but it finds declines both in the relative demand for low-skilled labor (using a shift-share analysis of the structure of output and thus ignoring another powerful source of the same effect, skill-biased technical change) and in the relative supply of low-skilled labor. It is not clear which of these declines was larger. It is striking, however, that among 17 OECD countries examined in OECD (1993), west Germany is the only one that shows a pronounced narrowing of wage differentials at the bottom of the distribution during the 1980s. Moreover, the high rates of unemployment for low-skilled workers strongly suggest that the narrowing of wage differentials was not merely an equilibrating response.

References

Abraham, Katherine G., and Susan N. Houseman, "Earnings Inequality in Germany," NBER Working Paper No. 4541 (Cambridge, Mass.: National Bureau for Economic Research, 1993).

Artus, Jacques R., "The Disequilibrium Real Wage Rate Hypothesis: An Empirical Evaluation," *Staff Papers*, International Monetary Fund, Vol. 31 (June 1984), pp. 249–302.

Bell, Linda A., "Wage Rigidity in West Germany: A Comparison with the U.S. Experience," *Federal Reserve Bank of New York Quarterly Review*, Vol. 11 (1986), pp. 11–19.

———, and Richard B. Freeman, "Does a Flexible Industry Wage Structure Increase Employment? The U.S. Experience," NBER Working Paper No. 1604 (Cambridge, Mass.: National Bureau for Economic Research, 1987).

Bellmann, Lutz, and Joachim Möller, "Institutional Influences on Inter-Industry Wage Differentials," *Regensburger Diskussionsbeiträge*, No. 257 (1993).

Bhaskar, V., "Wage Relativities and the Natural Range of Unemployment," *Economic Journal*, Vol. 100 (1990).

Börsch-Supan, Axel, "Panel Data Analysis of the Beveridge Curve: Is There a Macroeconomic Relation Between the Rate of Unemployment and the Vacancy Rate?" *Economica*, Vol. 58 (1991), pp. 279–97.

Budd, Alan, Paul Levine, and Peter Smith, "Long-Term Unemployment and the Shifting U-V Curve," *European Economic Review*, Vol. 31 (1987), pp. 296–305.

Burda, Michael C., and Jeffrey D. Sachs, "Institutional Aspects of High Unemployment in the Federal Republic of Germany," NBER Working Paper No. 2241 (Cambridge, Mass.: National Bureau for Economic Research, 1987).

---

[15]Nor is it clear how one should interpret trends in age differentials in Germany. Because the labor market situation is worse for older than younger people, the declining age differentials found by Abraham and Houseman might signal an appropriate responsiveness of wages to labor market conditions. However, more experienced people are also those most likely to be paid above-tariff wages, so that responsiveness in this area would not necessarily indicate a similar responsiveness in labor markets where tariff wages are binding.

Calmfors, Lars, "Centralization of Wage Bargaining and Macroeconomic Performance: A Survey," Seminar Paper No. 536 (Stockholm: Institute for International Economic Studies, 1993).

———, and John Driffill, "Bargaining Structure, Corporatism, and Macroeconomic Performance," *Economic Policy*, Vol. 6 (1988), pp. 13–61.

Carruth, Alan, and Claus Schnabel, "Empirical Modelling of Trade Union Growth in Germany, 1956–86: Traditional Versus Cointegration and Error Correction Methods," *Weltwirtschaftliches Archiv*, Vol. 126 (1990), pp. 326–46.

Coe, David T., "Nominal Wages, the NAIRU, and Wage Flexibility," *OECD Economic Studies*, Vol. 5 (1985), pp. 87–126.

———, and Thomas Krueger, "Why Is Unemployment So High at Full Capacity? The Persistence of Unemployment, the Natural Rate, and Potential Output in the Federal Republic of Germany," in *German Unification: Economic Issues*, IMF Occasional Paper 75 (Washington: International Monetary Fund, 1990).

Davis, Steven J., "Cross-Country Patterns of Changes in Relative Wages," *NBER Macroeconomics Annual* (Cambridge, Mass.: MIT Press, 1992).

Elmeskov, Jorgen, "High and Persistent Unemployment: Assessment of the Problem and Its Causes," Working Paper No. 32 (Paris: OECD Department of Economics, 1993).

Flanagan, Robert J., David W. Soskice, and Lloyd Ulmann, *Unionism, Economic Stabilization, and Incomes Policy: European Experience* (Washington: Brookings Institution, 1983).

Franz, Wolfgang, *Arbeitsmarktökonomik* (Berlin: Springer, 1991).

———, and Heinz König, "The Nature and Causes of Unemployment in the Federal Republic of Germany Since the 1970s: An Empirical Investigation," *Economica* (Supplement 1986), pp. S219–44.

Freeman, Richard, "Unionism and the Dispersion of Wages," *Industrial and Labour Relations Review*, Vol. 34 (1980).

———, "Labour Market Institutions and Economic Performance," *Economic Policy*, Vol. 4 (1988), pp. 64–78.

Grubb, David, and William Wells, "Employment Regulation and Patterns of Work in EC Countries," *OECD Economic Studies*, Vol. 21 (1993), pp. 7–58.

Gundlach, Erich, "Gibt es genügend Lohndifferenzierung in der Bundesrepublik Deutschland?" *Die Weltwirtschaft* (Tübingen), Vol. 1 (1986), pp. 74–78.

Jackman, Richard, and Stephen Roper, "Structural Unemployment," *Oxford Bulletin of Economics and Statistics*, Vol. 49 (1987), pp. 9–36.

Jaeger, Albert, and Martin Parkinson, "Testing for Hysteresis in Unemployment: An Unobserved Components Approach," *Empirical Economics*, Vol. 15 (1990), pp. 185–98.

Katz, Lawrence F., and Kevin M. Murphy, "Changes in Relative Wages, 1963–1987: Supply and Demand Factors," *Quarterly Journal of Economics*, Vol. 107 (1992), pp. 35–78.

Landmann, Oliver, and Jürgen Jerger, "Unemployment and the Real Wage Gap: A Reappraisal of the German Experience," *Weltwirtschaftliches Archiv*, Vol. 129 (1993), pp. 689–717.

OECD, *Employment Outlook* (Paris: Organization for Economic Cooperation and Development, 1991).

———, *Employment Outlook* (Paris: Organization for Economic Cooperation and Development, 1993).

——— (1994a), *Quarterly Labor Force Statistics*, No. 1 (Paris: Organization for Economic Cooperation and Development, 1994).

——— (1994b), *Employment Outlook* (Paris: Organization for Economic Cooperation and Development, 1994).

Paqué, Karl-Heinz, "Wage Gaps, Hysteresis and Structural Unemployment: The West German Labour Market in the Seventies and Eighties," Working Paper No. 358 (Kiel Institute of World Economics, 1989).

———, "Unemployment in West Germany: A Survey of Explanations and Policy Options," Working Paper No. 407 (Kiel Institute of World Economics, 1990).

Rowthorn, Robert E., "Centralization, Employment and Wage Dispersion," *Economic Journal*, Vol. 102 (1992), pp. 506–23.

Schultze, Charles L., "Real Wages, Real Wage Aspirations, and Unemployment in Europe," In *Barriers to European Economic Growth: A Transatlantic View* (Washington: Brookings Institution, 1987).

Soltwedel, Rüdiger, "Employment Problems in West Germany: The Role of Institutions, Labor Law, and Government Intervention," *Carnegie-Rochester Series on Public Policy*, Vol. 28 (1988), pp. 153–220.

Streeck, Wolfgang, "Industrial Relations in West Germany, 1980–1987," *Labour*, Vol. 2 (1988), pp. 3–44.

Zweimüller, Josef, and Erling Barth, "Bargaining Structure, Wage Determination, and Wage Dispersion in Six OECD Countries," *Kyklos*, Vol. 47 (1994), pp. 81–93.

IV   Fiscal Policy and Economic Growth

Karl Habermeier
with Steven Symansky[1]

Following German unification, the ratios of public revenue to GDP and expenditure to GDP rose sharply (Table 4-1). Further increases in expenditure are taking place in 1994–96 as the federal government begins to service the accumulated debt from currency conversion and privatization in east Germany. Expenditure on social benefits, notably on long-term care, pensions, and health, are also likely to increase faster than GDP in the years to come. In order to reduce the general government deficit to less than 2 percent of GDP as planned, the Government has already announced that it will continue to raise taxes, notably by reimposing a 7½ percent surcharge on wage and income taxes from the beginning of 1995. Contribution rates to the social security funds will also continue to increase gradually from their already high level.

The composition of fiscal measures affects growth and employment by affecting the incentives of households and businesses to save, invest, or work. Economic theory suggests that measures to raise revenue will discourage the activity being taxed, though taxes on consumption are less likely to discourage saving, investment, and work than are taxes on income and wealth. Similarly, most types of government spending, when carried beyond a certain point, are likely to dampen economic growth. In particular, generous welfare and unemployment compensation programs tend to reduce work effort and job search.

Empirical estimates of the effects of various fiscal policy variables on real activity in west Germany in 1960–90 show that lower fiscal deficits have been associated with faster growth. Furthermore, higher government expenditure and revenue ratios—that is, a larger public sector—have, on average, been associated with slower economic growth. A more disaggregated treatment supports the view that higher direct taxes have a more negative effect on growth than other means of raising revenue. Similarly, social transfer payments appear to be more detrimental to economic performance than subsidies to enterprises or public investment.

The effects of fiscal restructuring on macroeconomic performance are also assessed using simulations performed with the IMF's multi-country macroeconomic model (MULTIMOD).[2] Following a brief exposition of the channels through which fiscal policy operates in MULTIMOD, the consequences of an equal reduction in the ratios of both public revenue to GDP and public expenditure to GDP are considered. There is also a comparison of the macroeconomic effects of reducing taxes.

The results suggest that fiscal policy in Germany should aim to rectify the imbalance between revenue and expenditure measures in pursuing fiscal consolidation. Both the revenue and the expenditure ratios are already higher than those that would be compatible with robust medium-term economic growth, indicating a need to reduce the size of the public sector. The Government has recognized the need for changes in the structure of public finances. As currently enunciated, the strategy in this area emphasizes strict expenditure restraint accompanied by eventual reductions in taxes, as well as measures to reduce disincentives connected with the structure of the tax system.

Review of the Literature

There is a large literature on the relationship between public finances and other macroeconomic variables such as economic activity and inflation. One branch of this literature emphasizes the short-run stimulative effects, through higher effective demand, of increased public expenditure or lower taxation on economic activity. In contrast to this "Keynesian" tradition, another branch examines the effects of public revenue and expenditure on aggregate supply and longer-run growth. These "neoclassical" studies focus on how public sector acti-

---

[1]The MULTIMOD simulations in this section were provided by Steve Symansky.

[2]Recent work by Bartolini, Razin, and Symansky (1994) has extended MULTIMOD to capture the incentive effects of changes in tax and expenditure policy. See also Barro (1990).

Table 4-1. General Government Finances[1]
(In percent of GDP)

Historical data	1989	1990	1991	1992	1993	1994
Revenue	45.9	40.4	45.7	46.8	47.1	47.5
Expenditure	45.8	42.3	48.9	49.3	50.3	50.3
Financial balance	0.1	−1.9	−3.2	−2.6	−3.2	−2.8

Sources: Federal Ministry of Finance; and IMF staff calculations.
[1]Ratios for 1989 as a percentage of west German GDP; ratios for 1990–94 as a percentage of united German GDP.

vity affects the incentives facing households and businesses.[3]

Research on the longer-term consequences of public sector activity on economic growth have generally supported the hypothesis that increases in the size of the public sector, or higher tax rates, adversely affect economic activity. These results appear to hold in both time-series and cross-sectional studies.

Cebula and Scott (1992), using data for the United States for the 1957–84 period, show that a larger government deficit exerts a significant negative influence on economic growth. They also show that higher tax rates are associated with slower economic growth. On the basis of data for the United States for 1929–86, Peden (1991) finds that government expenditure, when it exceeds a certain percentage of GNP, reduces economic growth. Fardmanesh (1991), in a cross-sectional study of 21 developed countries over the period 1972–81, obtains the result that foreign trade taxes have the most adverse effects on growth, followed by income taxes and domestic excises. He also finds that cuts in current expenditure have no lasting effect on growth. Ahsan and others (1989), using the Granger bivariate model, find that in a cross-sectional sample of 24 industrialized countries, there is considerable support for bidirectional causality between government consumption expenditure and national income. Somewhat mixed results on the Australian experience are reported by Grossman (1988), with government expenditure showing a positive effect on growth but taxation a negative effect. Marsden (1983) argues, on the basis of data for a large cross-section of industrial and developing countries, that there is a pronounced negative correlation between taxation and growth.[4]

The results obtained by two other studies are somewhat more adverse to the hypothesis that higher taxation has an adverse effect on growth. Using a large cross-sectional sample of 63 countries, Koester and Kormendi (1989) find no negative relationship between marginal tax rates and economic growth when the relationship is controlled for the effects of per capita income on the growth rate. Garrison and Lee (1992), who extend the time period covered by Koester and Kormendi's data set, find no clear negative relationship between marginal tax rates and growth over the longer period. However, the time periods covered by both of these studies are far too short (1970–79 in the first study and 1970–84 in the second); moreover, a panel data approach would have been a more appropriate method of analysis than simply averaging the data over the sample period.

Results for Germany

There are a number of pitfalls in investigating the effects on economic growth of revenue and expenditure policy and the size of the public sector. First, economic activity is affected by many other factors besides fiscal policy. Monetary conditions, the international economic environment, the pace of technological innovation, and the age and skill structure of the population, as well as more general cultural and political factors, also influence the long-term rate of

---

[3]The rationale for the neoclassical approach is best summarized in a recent paper by King and Rebelo (1990). Their argument is that differences in the long-term growth rate of individual countries are explained by variations in the national policies that affect the incentives individuals have to accumulate physical and human capital. Courant (1987) and Boskin (1988) also discuss the interaction between fiscal policy and supply-side issues. Landau and Jorgenson (1986) examine the effects of tax policy on the incentive to innovate. Finally, see Barro (1990).

[4]Looking at the effect of taxation on growth over a period of centuries, a careful historical study by Hoffman (1991) argues that sharp increases in taxation in the early seventeenth century impeded the growth of agricultural productivity, preventing a recovery from the war damage of the previous century.

economic expansion. Most notably, the slowdown in economic growth in the 1970s is often attributed to the sharp increases in petroleum prices that occurred in 1973–74 and 1979.

Second, it is not obvious that causality runs from higher revenue and expenditure ratios to lower growth rather than the other way around. Slower economic growth may lead to calls for more government spending; the desire to contain the fiscal deficit may then lead to a higher revenue ratio as well.

It is clear that these issues cannot be definitively disentangled using econometric methods, all the more so as the growth rate of real GDP from year to year is erratic and hard to explain with any precision.[5]

Chart 4-1 summarizes the basic features of economic growth and public sector activity in west Germany over the sample period, which spans 1960 to 1990. A period of fast growth in the 1960s, during which the size of the public sector was relatively limited, was followed by a sharply growing public sector and considerably slower growth in the 1970s and early 1980s. These trends were reversed during the 1980s, when both the revenue and the expenditure ratios decreased and growth accelerated.

Simple regressions of the growth rate of real GDP and the ratios of overall revenue and expenditure to GDP, as well as of several subcategories of revenue and expenditure variables, are reported in Table 4-2. These estimates confirm the broad impression given by Chart 4-1 of a negative correlation between the scope of public sector activity and economic growth.

In order to reduce the influence of cyclical disturbances, the regressions were also modified by including a cyclical indicator that measures the percentage deviation of real GDP from a quadratic trend.[6] The results, which are presented in Table 4-3, are similar to those obtained by the simple regression. The causality tests reported below, which include a more general lag structure, represent a further approach to eliminating the influence of the cycle on the results.

On the whole, the coefficients reported in Tables 4-2 and 4-3 have the expected sign.[7] However,

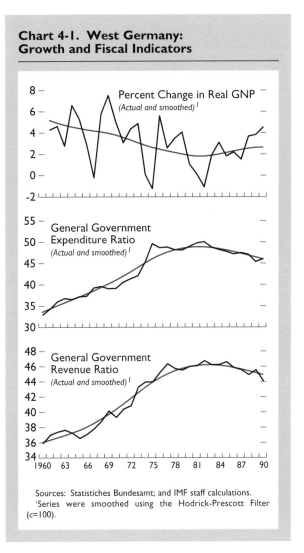

Chart 4-1. West Germany: Growth and Fiscal Indicators

Sources: Statistiches Bundesamt; and IMF staff calculations.
[1]Series were smoothed using the Hodrick-Prescott Filter (c=100).

---

[5]Augmented Dickey-Fuller tests on German real GDP in log levels fail to reject the hypothesis that the series is at least $I(1)$. Intuitively, this means that real GDP behaves much like a random walk.

[6]The inclusion of the cyclical indicator is intended to capture those effects on the growth rate that are purely transitory. An alternative approach is to smooth the growth rate of real GDP and the fiscal variables using the Hodrick-Prescott filter. This too had little effect on the sign and magnitude of the estimated coefficients.

[7]There is only one exception: the coefficient on indirect taxes is positive and significant at the 1 percent level.

the coefficients on tax revenues, subsidies, and investment expenditure are not significant at the 5 percent level. Also, several of the equations show evidence of slight positive serial correlation in the residuals. When these equations are "corrected" for the serial correlation using the Cochrane-Orcutt technique, the signs and magnitudes of most of the coefficients remain largely unchanged; furthermore, the estimated coefficients of serial correlation are smaller than 0.15 in many cases. Similarly, when a lagged value of the dependent variable is included in the equations, its coefficient is in no case significantly different from zero, and the coefficients on the fiscal variables are not materially affected, although their estimated standard errors increase somewhat.

These results suggest that the expansion of the public sector, which reached its peak in the early 1980s, was associated with slower economic growth

Table 4-2. Effect of Fiscal Variables on Economic Growth[1]

(Dependent variable: DLQ)

Explanatory Variable	Constant Term	Coefficient on Explanatory Variable	R^2	DW
RFB	0.039 (10.14)	0.00714 (4.00)	0.36	1.75
RR	0.137 (3.24)	−0.00249 (−2.53)	0.19	1.71
RT	0.112 (0.862)	−0.00329 (−0.628)	0.01	1.46
RTI	−0.182 (−2.41)	0.0160 (2.82)	0.22	1.60
RTD	0.113 (2.74)	−0.00709 (−2.01)	0.13	1.63
RTS	0.082 (4.26)	−0.00351 (−2.73)	0.21	1.69
RE	0.126 (4.27)	−0.00220 (−3.27)	0.28	1.72
REP	0.137 (4.19)	−0.00253 (−3.28)	0.28	1.72
REPU	0.138 (3.79)	−0.004 (−2.97)	0.24	1.69
RET	0.010 (3.82)	−0.00338 (−2.68)	0.20	1.70
RETS	0.122 (4.57)	−0.00602 (−3.47)	0.30	1.73
REC	0.134 (4.93)	−0.00575 (−3.84)	0.34	1.74
RES	0.039 (2.47)	−0.00473 (−0.56)	0.01	1.47
REI	0.474 (0.28)	0.00734 (1.54)	0.08	1.53

Sources: Federal Statistical Office; and IMF staff calculations.

[1]DLQ = logarithmic difference of real GDP, west Germany.
Ratios to GDP (in percent):
  RFB: general government financial balance;
  RR: general government revenue;
  REP: primary expenditure;
  REPU: primary expenditure, less social transfers;
  RT: tax revenue;
  RTI: indirect tax revenue;
  RTD: direct tax revenue;
  RTS: social security contributions;
  RE: general government expenditure;
  RET: transfer expenditure;
  RETS: social transfer expenditure;
  REC: government consumption expenditure;
  RES: subsidy expenditure;
  REI: investment expenditure.

and that growth picked up again in the 1980s as the size of the public sector decreased. Moreover, the increasing deficits seen in the 1970s were associated with a deceleration in economic activity.

Although the relative magnitude of the estimated coefficients is subject to great uncertainty, the estimates suggest that among revenue instruments, di-

rect taxes are most harmful to growth and social security contributions are less harmful; indirect taxes appear to exert a positive influence, perhaps by reducing the attractiveness of consumption relative to saving. On the expenditure side, subsidies and public investment expenditure seem to have little measurable effect on growth rates, while public consumption has a strong negative impact. Consistent with the view that incentives matter, social transfers have the largest negative effect of any expenditure category.

Looking to the future, a straightforward application of these results suggests that the sharp expansion of the public sector since unification may considerably reduce the rate of economic growth. Specifically, an increase in the ratio of noninterest expenditures or overall revenues by 1 percentage point will lead to a reduction in the growth rate of about 0.2 percentage point. If the relationship were truly linear, the almost 10 percentage point increase in the size of the public sector that is expected between 1989 and 1995 should reduce the long-term rate of economic growth by about 2 percentage points. A much more conservative estimate was obtained by subtracting two standard errors from the absolute value of the coefficients; in this case, the rate of economic growth would be reduced by between ¼ and 1 percent annually.

Tests of "causation" were also performed to obtain a clearer sense of the dynamic relationships among real GNP and fiscal variables and to examine whether other factors, such as the real price of oil, played an important role in explaining the behavior of the growth rate. Using the Geweke variant of the Granger bivariate model (Table 4-4), it was shown that price-adjusted general government revenues both caused and were caused by real output but that there was no causation among price-adjusted general government expenditures and real output.[8] However, once general government expenditures were adjusted for interest expenditure (which is related to the debt dynamics) and for social transfers (which are cyclical to a considerable extent), the remaining "structural" expenditures cause real output but are not caused by it. Finally, it was found that the real price of oil (in deutsche mark terms) neither causes nor is caused by real output.[9]

Thus, the power of oil prices to explain movements in real output in Germany appears to be smaller than commonly assumed, while the relation-

---

[8]The tests were conducted using three lags and two leads.

[9]The tests reported here were performed on log-level data; essentially the same results were obtained when log differences were used for real output and ratios to GNP were used for the fiscal variables.

Table 4-3. Effect of Fiscal Variables on Economic Growth, with Cyclical Indicator[1]
(Dependent variable: DLQ)

Explanatory Variable	Constant Term	Coefficient on Explanatory Variable	Cyclical Indicator	R^2	DW
RFB	0.038	0.00607	0.00260	0.47	1.73
	(10.7)	(3.52)	(2.31)		
RR	0.119	−0.00205	0.00315	0.35	1.57
	(3.03)	(−2.24)	(2.57)		
RT	0.189	−0.00638	0.00404	0.27	1.44
	(1.63)	(−1.36)	(3.11)		
RTI	−0.144	0.01342	0.00304	0.37	1.47
	(−2.05)	(2.49)	(2.52)		
RTD	0.118	−0.00741	0.00376	0.36	1.56
	(3.28)	(−2.42)	(3.16)		
RTS	0.073	−0.00285	0.00303	0.36	1.56
	(4.05)	(−2.35)	(2.48)		
RE	0.111	−0.00184	0.00288	0.41	1.63
	(3.98)	(−2.89)	(2.45)		
REP	0.124	−0.00221	0.00301	0.43	1.65
	(4.16)	(−3.13)	(2.70)		
REPU	0.136	−0.00390	0.00356	0.45	1.66
	(4.32)	(−3.34)	(3.23)		
RET	0.088	−0.00276	0.00306	0.35	1.59
	(3.59)	(−2.33)	(2.50)		
RETS	0.104	−0.00480	0.00250	0.39	1.64
	(3.88)	(−2.73)	(2.02)		
REC	0.120	−0.00492	0.00272	0.46	1.66
	(4.63)	(−3.44)	(2.41)		
RES	0.042	−0.00605	0.00372	0.24	1.39
	(3.00)	(−0.80)	(2.87)		
REI	0.025	0.00177	0.00341	0.23	1.30
	(1.37)	(0.35)	(2.29)		

Sources: Federal Statistical Office; and IMF staff calculations.
[1]DLQ = logarithmic difference of real GDP, west Germany.
Ratios to GDP, in percent:
   RFB: general government financial balance;
   RR: general government revenue;
   REP: primary expenditure;
   REPU: primary expenditure, less social transfers;
   RT: tax revenue;
   RTI: indirect tax revenue;
   RTD: direct tax revenue;
   RTS: social security contributions;
   RE: general government expenditure;
   RET: transfer expenditure;
   RETS: social transfer expenditure;
   REC: government consumption expenditure;
   RES: subsidy expenditure;
   REI: investment expenditure.

ships between fiscal variables and economic activity are considerably more pronounced. Although no firm conclusions can be drawn on the basis of such a narrow investigation, the results lend some support to the hypothesis put forward by King and Rebelo that differences in institutions and policies are a primary cause of variations in growth performance over time and across countries.

Results from an International Cross-Section

Additional support for the results presented above was obtained by estimating the effect of the ratios of current revenue and current expenditure to GDP on the growth rate of real GDP for a sample of industrialized countries covering 1964 to

Table 4-4. Geweke Tests for Causality[1]

	F-Statistic	Causality
Expenditure → Real GDP	1.77	No
Real GDP → Expenditure	1.38	No
Adj. expenditure → Real GDP[2]	3.24	Yes
Real GDP → Adj. expenditure[2]	2.51	No
Revenue → Real GDP	6.26	Yes
Real GDP → Revenue	4.23	Yes
Oil price → Real GDP	1.11	No
Real GDP → Oil price	0.38	No

Sources: Federal Statistical Office; and IMF staff calculations.

[1]The critical values for rejection of the null hypothesis of "no causality" are 2.74 at the 5 percent level and 4.17 at the 1 percent level.

[2]Expenditure excluding interest and social transfers.

Table 4-5. Effect of Fiscal Variables on Growth in Selected Industrial Countries[1]

	Current Expenditure	Current Revenue	Financial Balance
Austria	−0.2	−0.3	0.6
Belgium	−0.2	−0.2	...
Canada	−0.2	−0.3	0.5
Finland	−0.3	−0.4	0.6
France	−0.2	−0.3	0.1
Italy	−0.1	−0.2	0.4
Norway	−0.1	−0.1	...
Sweden	−0.1	−0.1	0.1[2]
United Kingdom	−0.1[2]	−0.3	0.2[2]

Sources: *OECD Economic Outlook*; and IMF staff calculations.

[1]Estimated effect of 1 percentage point increase in fiscal variable on the growth rate.

[2]Not significant at 5 percent level.

Chart 4-2. Major Industrial Countries: Growth and Fiscal Indicators

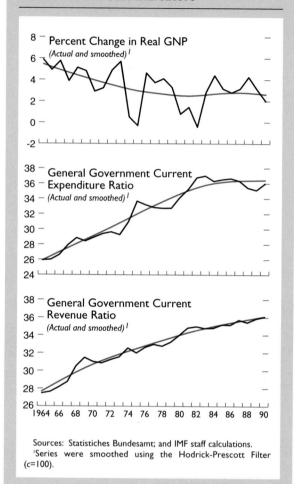

Sources: Statistiches Bundesamt; and IMF staff calculations.
[1]Series were smoothed using the Hodrick-Prescott Filter (c=100).

1991.[10] As shown in Table 4-5, the results are generally consistent with the findings for Germany: an improvement in the financial balance is associated with faster growth, while higher revenue and expenditure ratios are related to slower growth.[11]

In order to reduce the influence of the international transmission of the business cycle on the results, the data for the individual countries were aggregated using the weights from the IMF's World Economic Outlook exercise.[12] The aggregated data are shown in Chart 4-2. Again, the increase in the size of the public sector that took place from the 1960s to the early 1980s was associated with slowing growth. Unlike Germany, however, there was no reduction in the share of the public sector in the 1980s and no revival of economic growth.

These observations are confirmed by econometric estimates. Table 4-6 reports the results obtained by regressing the growth rate of real GDP on aggregate current revenue, aggregate current expenditure, and public saving ratios. Again, the signs and magni-

---

[10]The sample comprises Austria, Belgium, Canada, Finland, France, Germany, Italy, Japan, Norway, Sweden, the United Kingdom, and the United States. These countries account for more than half of world output for most of the sample period.

[11]The magnitude of the coefficients is little affected by including cyclical indicators in the regressions, or by first smoothing the underlying data using the Hodrick-Prescott filter.

[12]These weights are based on estimated purchasing power parity.

Table 4-6. Major Industrial Countries: Effect of Fiscal Variables on Growth[1]

(Dependent variable: DLQ)

Explanatory Variable	Constant Term	Coefficient on Explanatory Variable	R^2	DW
RPS	0.031 (10.32)	0.00690 (3.24)	0.29	1.28
RRC	0.157 (4.22)	−0.00379 (−3.35)	0.30	1.56
REC	0.127 (5.03)	−0.00290 (−3.75)	0.35	1.50

Sources: Federal Statistical Office; and IMF staff calculations.

[1]DLQ = logarithmic difference of real GDP, aggregated. Ratios to GDP (in percent):

RPS: general government saving;

RRC: general government current revenue;

REC: general government current expenditure.

Table 4-7. Major Industrial Countries: Geweke Tests for Causality[1]

	F-Statistic	Causality
Current expenditure → Real GDP	12.03	Yes
Real GDP → Current expenditure	4.64	Yes
Current revenue → Real GDP	12.17	Yes
Real GDP → Current revenue	2.87	Yes
Oil price → Real GDP	3.51	Yes
Real GDP → Oil price	2.30	No

Sources: Federal Statistical Office; and IMF staff calculations.

[1]The critical values for rejection of the null hypothesis of "no causality" are 2.81 at the 5 percent level and 4.34 at the 1 percent level.

tudes of the elasticities are consistent with the German experience.

Finally, the pattern of "causation" among real GDP and three other variables—real government revenue, real government expenditure, and the real oil price—was examined using the Geweke test. The results are summarized in Table 4-7. Output both "causes" revenue and is caused by it; in addition, the strength of the effect of revenues on output is significantly greater than the other way around. A similar pattern emerges for government expenditure. Finally, oil prices cause output but not vice versa; thus, the effect of oil prices appears to be more pronounced for the industrial countries as a group than for an individual country such as Germany.

Incorporating Distortionary Taxes and Spending into MULTIMOD[13]

This section outlines the effects of tax and expenditure policies on consumption, labor and capital income, and the government budget constraint, the main channels through which taxes and spending affect economic behavior. Based on these considerations, Bartolini, Razin, and Symansky (1994) added several new equations to MULTIMOD and modified a number of others.[14]

The labor market segment of the revised MULTIMOD consists of three behavioral equations governing price setting, wage setting, and unemployment. The equations describe cyclical fluctuations of unemployment around its natural level, which is taken as largely exogenous and is regarded as the long-run outcome of a search-bargain framework, such as that of Pissarides (1985). Although the framework is not specified as a full-fledged bargaining model, it preserves the intuition that there is a positive link between equilibrium unemployment and a broadly defined labor income tax, a result that is also well supported empirically.[15] The model, however, does not incorporate the effect of unemployment benefits on equilibrium unemployment.

The wage-setting equation fixes the long-run growth of real consumption wages as a function of average productivity growth and other structural factors (such as relative bargaining power and the target real wage), which are absorbed into the constant term. Taxes on goods and services, such as the value-added tax (VAT), enter this equation through their effect on the consumer price level. The unemployment equation combines labor demand and labor supply elements, which in turn reflect the effects of taxes on labor income and consumption, with an element that captures the effect of taxation on the natural rate of unemployment. Finally, the price-setting equation is of a standard form and assumes that prices are a markup on unit labor costs.

In addition to affecting the supply side of the economy through their effect on real wages and unemployment, taxes and government expenditure also influence consumption and investment decisions, the

---

[13]The model simulations were conducted by Steve Symansky.

[14]A complete description of MULTIMOD may be found in Masson, Symansky, and Meredith (1990).

[15]See, for instance, Adams and Coe (1990), Coe and Krueger (1990), and Lockwood and Manning (1993).

Table 4-8. Macroeconomic Effects of Balanced Revenue and Expenditure Reduction
(Percentage deviation from baseline levels, unless otherwise noted)

	1996	1997	1998	1999	2000	Long Term
Real GDP	0.9	1.4	1.6	1.3	1.3	0.8
Unemployment rate[1]	−0.3	−0.7	−1.0	−1.1	−1.1	−0.6
GNP deflator	−0.7	−1.2	−1.6	−1.5	−1.1	−0.1
Wages	−0.7	−1.2	−1.2	−0.7	−0.2	1.0
Real short-term rate[1]	0.4	0.1	−0.8	−1.1	−0.9	—
Real long-term rate[1]	0.1	−0.2	−0.5	−0.5	−0.3	—
Exchange rate (effective)	−4.5	−4.7	−4.8	−4.7	−4.2	−2.6
Current account balance[2]	7.1	21.0	33.9	46.9	46.8	...

Source: IMF staff calculations.
[1]Percentage point deviation from baseline level.
[2]Billions of deutsche mark.

dynamics of government debt, and various national income and price deflator identities. The effect of VAT on the consumer price index has already been mentioned. The intertemporal budget constraints of private households, business enterprises, and government were each modified to reflect the effects of the three categories of taxes that are distinguished in the model.

Balanced Reduction in Revenue and Expenditure

The model as modified by Bartolini, Razin, and Symansky was used to examine the macroeconomic effects of equal reductions in the ratios of revenue and expenditure to GDP. It was assumed that the revenue ratio would be reduced by 1 percentage point each year over a four-year period beginning in 1996, with the reductions equally divided between wage and consumption taxes. This change was matched by an equivalent cut in expenditure, also spread over four years. Not taking into account the feedback effect of these changes on macroeconomic variables, these actions would imply an unchanged general government deficit.

The principal results are summarized in Table 4-8, which gives deviations from the baseline projection. All in all, the medium-term effects of a balanced reduction in revenue and expenditure are highly favorable, with real GDP some 1¼ percent above the baseline level in the year 2000, the GNP deflator about 1 percent lower than the baseline, and the unemployment rate 1 percentage point lower.

Much of the positive impact of this restructuring on GDP can be attributed to the stimulation of domestic demand, particularly consumption and in-

vestment. Nonetheless, the beneficial spillover effects on other countries and the real depreciation of the deutsche mark, partly induced by lower domestic interest rates, contribute to an increase in net exports and an improvement in the current account balance by about 1 percent of GDP.

Tax Restructuring

This section examines the macroeconomic effects of a revenue-neutral change in the tax system, one in which a reduction in one category of taxation is offset by an increase of equivalent size in another category of taxation. This type of policy change, which may also be called tax substitution, is of interest because it allows efficiency gains to be captured without increasing the budget deficit.

Table 4-9 illustrates the effect in MULTIMOD of reducing taxes on labor income by 2 percent of GDP, compensated by an equivalent increase in taxes on goods and services. The initial impact of this policy change on real GDP is negative but small. In the longer run, the effect is positive. This reflects the negative influence on consumption of higher taxes on goods and services; in conjunction with the dampening influence on wages of lower taxes on labor income, this enhances the incentives for investment. The higher level of GDP, and the lower level of wage taxes, is also reflected in a lower unemployment rate. As expected, the effect on prices is positive, but this is later reversed by the reduction in wages relative to the baseline.

For the purposes of illustrating the effects in MULTIMOD of changes in tax policy, simulations were run in which each of the three categories of taxes in the model was reduced, other things equal,

Table 4-9. Macroeconomic Effects of Tax Restructuring[1]
(Percentage deviation from baseline levels unless otherwise noted)

	1997	1998	1999	2000	Long Term
Tax substitution[1]					
Taxes on goods and services for taxes on labor income					
Real GDP	−0.2	−0.1	0.2	0.4	0.7
GDP deflator	0.5	−0.1	−0.5	−0.8	−0.9
Wages	−0.7	−1.3	−1.8	−2.1	−2.0
Unemployment rate[2]	0.1	—	−0.1	−0.2	−0.6
Tax reduction[3]					
Taxes on labor income					
Real GDP	0.5	0.7	0.8	0.8	0.3
Unemployment rate[2]	−0.1	−0.3	−0.5	−0.6	−0.5
Taxes on capital					
Real GDP	0.4	0.5	0.4	0.4	1.3
Unemployment rate[2]	−0.1	−0.2	−0.2	−0.2	−0.1
Taxes on goods and services					
Real GDP	0.7	0.9	0.7	0.4	—
Unemployment rate[2]	−0.2	−0.4	−0.5	−0.5	—

Source: IMF staff calculations.
[1]Reduction in one category of taxation (by 2 percent of GDP in 1997) offset by an equivalent increase in another category of taxation.
[2]Percentage point deviation from baseline level.
[3]By the equivalent of 2 percent of GDP in 1997.

by the equivalent of 2 percent of GDP. The results of this experiment need to be interpreted with caution, as the simulations are invariant to the level of the deficit in the baseline. In reality, it is likely that the effect of a tax reduction depends not only on the size of the cut itself but on the credibility and sustainability of fiscal policy before the cut. With this caveat, the conclusion is that reductions in tax rates lead to increases in real GDP and lower the unemployment rate. Interestingly, an alleviation of capital taxation produces the largest positive effect on real GDP in the long run, possibly suggesting that further efforts to streamline and reduce taxes on business capital may be desirable.

References

Adams, Charles, and David T. Coe, "A Systems Approach to Estimating the Natural Rate of Unemployment and Potential Output for the United States," *Staff Papers*, International Monetary Fund, Vol. 37 (1990), pp. 232–93.

Ahsan, Syed, and others, "Causality Between Government Consumption Expenditure and National Income," *Public Finance*, No. 2 (1989).

Barro, Robert, "Government Spending in a Simple Model of Endogenous Growth," *Journal of Political Economy* (October 1990).

Bartolini, L., A. Razin, and S. Symansky, "G-7 Fiscal Restructuring in the 1990s: Macroeconomic Effects" (unpublished; Washington: International Monetary Fund, 1994).

Boskin, Michael, "Tax Policy and Economic Growth: Lessons from the 1980s," *Journal of Economic Perspectives* (Fall 1988), pp. 71–97.

Cebula, Richard, and Gerald Scott, "Fiscal Policies and Growth: An Extension," *Rivista Internazionale di Scienze Economiche e Commerciali* (January 1992), pp. 91–94.

Coe, David T., and Thomas Krueger, "Why Is Unemployment So High at Full Capacity? The Persistence of Unemployment, the Natural Rate, and Potential Output in the Federal Republic of Germany," in *German Unification: Economic Issues*, IMF Occasional Paper 75 (Washington: International Monetary Fund, 1990).

Courant, Paul, "Fiscal Policy and European Economic Growth," in *Barriers to European Economic Growth: A Transatlantic View* (Washington: Brookings Institution, 1987).

Fardmanesh, Mohsin, "Economic Growth and Alternative Deficit-Reducing Tax Increases and Expenditure Cuts: A Cross-Sectional Study," *Public Choice* (February 1991).

Garrison, Charles, and Feng-Yao Lee, "Taxation, Aggregate Activity and Economic Growth," *Economic Inquiry* (January 1992).

Grossman, Philip, "Growth in Government and Economic Growth: The Australian Experience," Australian Economic Papers (June 1988).

Hoffman, Philip, "Land Rents and Agricultural Productivity: The Paris Basin, 1450–1789," *Journal of Economic History* (December 1991).

King, Robert, and Sergio Rebelo, "Public Policy and Economic Growth: Developing Neoclassical Implications," *Journal of Political Economy* (October 1990).

Koester, Reinhard, and Roger Kormendi, "Taxation, Aggregate Activity, and Economic Growth: Cross-Country Evidence on Some Supply-Side Hypotheses," *Economic Inquiry* (July 1989).

Landau, Ralph, and Dale Jorgenson, *Technology and Economic Policy* (New York: Ballinger, 1986).

Lockwood, B., and A. Manning, "Wage Setting and the Tax System: Theory and Evidence for the United Kingdom," *Journal of Public Economics*, Vol. 52 (1993), pp. 1–29.

Marsden, Keith, "Taxes and Growth," *Finance and Development* (September 1983).

Masson, Paul, Steven Symansky, and S. Meredith, *MULTIMOD Mark II: A Revised and Extended Model*, IMF Occasional Paper 71 (Washington: International Monetary Fund, 1990).

Peden, Edgar, "Productivity in the United States and Its Relationship to Government Activity: An Analysis of 57 Years, 1929–1986," *Public Choice* (February 1991).

Pissarides, Christopher, "Taxes, Subsidies, and Equilibrium Unemployment," *Review of Economic Studies*, Vol. 52 (1985), pp. 121–33.

V Indicators of Monetary Conditions

Robert Corker

The overshooting of the broad money target in recent years begs the question as to whether there is a serious risk of a pickup in inflation down the road. This chapter tries to shed some light on this issue by providing an empirical analysis of different monetary indicators. It finds that both money growth and a monetary conditions index (MCI), constructed as a weighted average of real short-term interest rates and the real effective exchange rate, have in the past provided useful early warning signals for inflation. Nevertheless, neither indicator would have predicted developments in inflation around the turn of the decade very well—perhaps not a surprising result, given the unprecedented nature of the demand shock to the west German economy associated with unification. During 1992–93, when money growth increased significantly, the MCI indicated that monetary conditions remained fairly tight. Since there were good reasons to suspect that the monetary data were distorted by special factors, the behavior of the MCI at this time suggests that the policy of cutting official interest rates during 1993 and the first half of 1994, even in the face of further surges in monetary growth, was appropriate. The validity of this policy is also borne out by the subsequent slowdown in monetary growth in the second half of 1994 and the favorable evolution of wage and price inflation.

Background

The conduct of monetary policy in Germany is predicated on the view that there is a long-run relationship between money growth and inflation. An explanation for this relationship, which underpins the calculation of the Bundesbank's annual monetary target, begins with the Quantity Theory identity:

$$MV = PY \qquad (1)$$

where M is the money stock (M3 in the target definition), V is money velocity, P is the average price level, and Y is real income. On the assumption that velocity follows a predictable path and that real income growth is constrained to the potential growth of supply in the long run, it is then possible to translate a specific inflation goal (price stability) into an annual target for monetary growth.[1] By adhering to the target, monetary conditions would tighten (in the sense that the quantity of money would be lower than normally warranted by the nominal value of transactions in the economy) if actual inflation were higher than the objective or actual output growth were above potential. In this way, while the objective of monetary policy would be price stability, the framework would in principle allow monetary conditions to vary in a countercyclical manner.

From an empirical perspective, this framework assumes that causality runs from money to inflation—although the route of causality may be indirect, through other variables such as incomes, exchange rates, or asset prices—and that velocity movements are predictable (money demand is stable).[2] Studies tend to confirm the existence of a positive causal link between developments in money and future prices for Germany. In addition, there is evidence—although the consensus is not unchallenged in the literature—that money demand was stable, at least in the period up to unification in mid-1990.[3] However, the continuation of this stability in recent years is more contentious, with some evidence that, at the very least, there has been a once-off break around unification in the hitherto stable path of velocity. See Box 1, as well as Chart 5-1 and Table 5-1.

More generally, even if money demand is stable, practical use of a target framework requires that the starting point for basing the money target can be assessed properly. In effect, a judgment has to be made as to what extent the target growth rate of money

---

[1]In 1994, for example, the target was based on an objective of 2 percent inflation, a decline in trend velocity of 1 percent a year, and potential growth of 2½ percent a year, giving an indicative monetary growth target of 5½ percent. The actual target was expressed as a range (4–6 percent) with adjustments added for target overshooting in previous years. See Deutsche Bundesbank, *Monthly Report* (January 1994), pp. 17–21.

[2]Note that equation (1) always holds true by identity and can be consistent with an entirely different causal ordering: inflation could originate from a completely separate process and money adjust subsequently to accommodate a higher price level.

[3]See, for example, von Hagen (1993) and Cassard, Lane, and Masson (1994).

Box 1. Stability of the Demand for M3

The stability of the demand for M3 can be tested using the two-stage estimation procedure of Engle and Granger (1987). This procedure tests first for the existence of a stable, long-run statistical relationship among money, income, and interest rates. Such tests confirm that money was cointegrated with money and income in the pre-unification era. Moreover, adding a time trend to the relationship suggests that the income elasticity of real money demand was unity or, put another way, that money velocity fluctuated about a stable trend (Table 5-1). The trend was downward at an estimated rate of about 1½ percent a year, or a little more than the amount the Bundesbank usually factors into its calculation of the monetary target range. Either short- or long-term interest rates, with correctly signed coefficients, can also be legitimately included in the cointegrating relationship.

If the sample period is extended beyond unification, the cointegration results underpinning the existence of a long-run stability in money demand break down unless a sizable one-off increase in velocity is allowed for. The shift in velocity, which is estimated to have occurred in 1990, could reflect a combination of unusual portfolio shifts around the time of unification as well as data measurement errors. The size and permanence of the velocity shift is sensitive to data splicing assumptions and the specification of dummy variables in the regression analysis. For example, analysis in the 1994 *OECD Economic Survey* for Germany assumes that a shift in money demand occurs after 1990, and, partly as a result, the analysis comes to more sanguine conclusions about the underlying stability of money demand. However, developments in velocity suggest that unusual portfolio shifts probably began ahead of unification, which occurred in the middle of 1990.

Nevertheless, it should be stressed that it is too early to conclude whether there has been a permanent break in trend velocity or whether the rapid monetary growth through early 1994 was in the process of reversing an earlier portfolio shift (Chart 5-1, top panel). This issue has, of course, important implications for the interpretation of postunification monetary growth. If the velocity shift was permanent, velocity would have been well below trend and a sizable monetary overhang would have existed by early 1994. But if a reversal of an earlier portfolio shift was taking place (or a new portfolio shift was occurring),

the rapid monetary growth through the early part of 1994 would probably pose little concern for medium-term inflation.

In the second stage of the analysis, an error correction equation for money demand is estimated. This equation exhibits parameter instability in the postunification period, even if a shift in trend velocity is factored into the long-run properties of the equation (see below). The equation begins to break down in the second half of 1992 (Chart 5-1, lower panel). This could, in part, reflect the increased variance of monetary growth owing to the large bouts of currency intervention during the two ERM crises. The equation breaks down completely in the first quarter of 1994 as it fails to predict the surge in M3 growth—although special factors, notably changes in the taxation of interest income, may again provide part of the explanation.

Money Demand Equation

$$\Delta\log(M) = 0.659\ \Delta\log(M_{-1}) - 0.132R + 0.141\ \Delta\log(Y)$$
$$(8.3) \qquad\qquad (2.3) \qquad (2.6)$$

$$+ 0.112\ \log(V_{-1}/V^*_{-1}) + 0.006,$$
$$(2.4) \qquad\qquad (3.5)$$

where $V = PY/M$ and $V^* = -0.015TT + 0.200R + 29.897 + 0.066DUM$.

OLS: 1971:2–1989:4; $R^2 = 0.508$; $DW = 1.96$; $DH = -0.109$; $AUTO = 16.46\ (11.1)$; $FORE(17) = 79.79\ (27.6)$.

The variables are M for money stock (M3); P for the GDP deflator; Y for real GDP; V for velocity; R for three-month money market rates; TT for a time trend; and DUM for a shift dummy taking the value 1 from 1990:1 onward. The symbol Δ represents a fourth difference ($\Delta X = X - X{-}4$). The reported test statistics are DH for Durbin's H-statistic; $AUTO$ for a test for serial correlation of up to lag five; and $FORE(17)$ for an out-of-sample parameter stability test for the period 1990:1–1994:1.

In summary, it is difficult to avoid the conclusion that money demand has exhibited instability since unification. However, the nature of the instability and the implications for the interpretation of monetary growth are unlikely to become clear for some time.

should allow for any earlier monetary overhang. As a case in point, the added measurement uncertainties caused by unification make it unclear whether the ensuing increase in monetary growth reflects over-loose monetary conditions or a return of velocity to trend.

The monetary framework assumes nothing specific about the transmission channels from money to prices. In principle, several channels are possible. From the domestic side, the effect might be through

interest rates and their impact on output, as in the conventional IS-LM framework. Where a broad money aggregate is considered, more direct wealth effects might also come into play and, in some cases, the impact might be felt first in asset markets.[4] From the external side, there might be a link

---

[4]Schinasi (1994), for example, notes that this phenomenon played an important role in the latest business cycle in a number of countries.

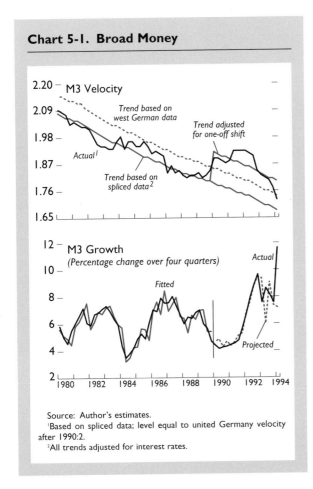

Chart 5-1. Broad Money

2.20 — M3 Velocity

2.09 —

Trend based on
west German data

Trend adjusted
for one-off shift

1.98 —

Actual[1]

1.87 —

Trend based on
spliced data[2]

1.76 —

1.65 —

12 — M3 Growth
(Percentage change over four quarters)

Actual

10 —

Fitted

8 —

6 —

4 —

Projected

2 —
1980 1982 1984 1986 1988 1990 1992 1994

Source: Author's estimates.
[1]Based on spliced data; level equal to united Germany velocity after 1990:2.
[2]All trends adjusted for interest rates.

between monetary growth and the exchange rate, which has a direct impact on domestic prices via import costs and prices and an indirect effect via changes in trade volumes.

Thus, an alternative to basing the monetary framework on a particular money aggregate would be to gauge monetary conditions from developments in other financial indicators such as interest rates, exchange rates, and asset prices, which may play more direct roles in determining output and inflation. If money demand and other behavioral relationships in the economy are stable, such indicators would convey information about monetary conditions similar to that provided by the monetary aggregates. It is conceivable that if money demand were behaving less predictably, alternative financial indicators could provide more reliable information.

In a number of countries, including Canada, New Zealand, and Sweden, where developments in domestic monetary aggregates have been difficult to interpret, increasing reliance has been placed on financial indicator variables. In the case of Canada, an MCI consisting of a weighted average of interest

rates and the effective exchange rate has proved to be a helpful indicator of inflationary pressures.[5] The weighting in the index reflects the relative partial impacts on inflation or output of each financial indicator over a period of about two years. The rationale for combining the two elements rests upon the fact that the domestic indicator of monetary conditions (interest rates) and the external indicator (exchange rates) can, in practice, convey independent information about monetary conditions. For example, an increase in interest rates that was accompanied by exchange rate appreciation might have a greater effect on output and prices than an interest rate rise alone.

In what follows, a monetary indicator is constructed for Germany. This index is compared with M3 as a predictor of future inflation, and the analysis is used to provide an assessment of recent monetary conditions.

A First Look at the Data

By international standards, German inflation has been low in the past few decades. Annual increases in the GDP deflator (one of the broadest measures of inflation) reached 8 percent in the early 1970s but then declined to about 4 percent in the second half of that decade (Chart 5-2). After picking up briefly at the turn of the decade, inflation slowed again and for most of the 1980s was contained in a 1–3 percent band. More recently, inflation in west Germany showed a persistent rise from its low point in 1988 of 1½ percent to a peak of 4½ percent in 1992—a period that included unification in 1990. Inflation has since abated: by end-1993, it had eased to about 3 percent and fell further during 1994.

From inspection of Chart 5-2, it is clear that several of the turning points in inflation were preceded by changes in the growth of broad money (M3) in the same direction. The lag appears to be a couple of years. Thus, the slowdowns in inflation in the mid-1970s and the early 1980s were both preceded by sharp decelerations in money growth, while the pickup in inflation in the late 1980s was preceded by a pickup in money growth in the mid-1980s. However, the most recent rise in inflation is less obviously related to earlier money growth developments—although this period is more difficult to interpret because of the disruptions to key data stemming from unification. Indeed, money growth was on a *declining* path from 1987 to around 1991.

Two other potential factors behind historical movements in inflation are also included in

---

[5]See Freedman (1994).

Table 5-1. Cointegration Tests: Money, Income, and Interest Rates[1]

	Test Statistics	
	DF	ADF
Pre-unification data (1970:1–1989:4)		
Model		
$M - P = 1.69Y - 0.32R - 8.07$	5.32**	3.02
$M - P = 1.06Y - 0.16R + 0.013TT - 30.92$	4.30**	3.38*
$V = -0.015TT + 0.14R + 30.00$	3.97*	3.35*
$V = -0.015TT + 30.42$	3.75**	3.67**
Full data set (1970:1–1994:4)		
$V = -0.012TT + 25.32$	2.22	3.09*
$V = -0.012TT + 0.47R + 25.05$	2.62	2.93
$V = -0.015TT + 30.50 + .073DUM$	3.68*	4.22**
$V = -0.015TT + 0.20R + 29.90 + .066DUM$	3.89*	3.84**

Source: IMF staff estimates.

[1]The variables are as follows: M, broad money (M3); P, the GDP deflator; Y, real GDP; V, money velocity; TT, a time trend; and R, three-month money market rates. Variables other than interest rates are in logarithms and, for the period up to unification, refer to west Germany only. Data on velocity (V) refer to united Germany, with estimates before unification based on west German data. See Appendix for splicing assumptions. DF stands for the Dickey-Fuller statistic and ADF its augmented version with four lags. A single asterisk denotes significance (likely cointegration) at the 10 percent level and a double asterisk denotes significance at the 5 percent level.

Chart 5-2. The first, denoted the output gap, measures the percentage deviation of real GDP in west Germany from its trend level.[6] These deviations appear broadly correlated with inflation. In particular, the climb down from the peak of inflation in 1980 to the low levels in the rest of that decade corresponds to a period in which output generally persisted at a level below normal capacity. The more recent increase in inflation took place against a shift to above-normal capacity utilization—particularly as the west German economy boomed in the immediate postunification period. As the recession hit in 1992–93, inflation slowed.

The second factor, changes in import prices, also appears to bear some loose correlation with the historical movements in inflation—although the visual evidence is less strong for west Germany than it is for other countries. In particular, it can be seen that inflation picked up temporarily around the times of the oil price hikes of 1973–74 and 1979–80, while the fall in inflation to its low of about 1 percent in 1987 appears to have been helped by the collapse in oil prices in the middle of the 1980s.

Determinants of Inflation: Evidence from VARs

This section utilizes vector autoregressive (VAR) models to evaluate the predictive roles of various monetary indicators in the inflation process. VAR models are based on regressions of each variable on lagged values of itself and the other variables in the system. They have the advantage of permitting an evaluation of the properties of the data without imposing prior restrictions suggested by economic theory or by policy reaction rules. However, the analysis is subject to practical constraints, such as limits on degrees of freedom and problems of multicollinearity in the data, and the results can be quite sensitive to changes in model specification. A key metric of the importance of the variables is provided by a decomposition of the VAR system's forecast error variance for inflation.[7] Further information is provided by examining the response of each variable to random perturbations in each equation (the "impulse responses").

Pre-unification Data

The analysis of VAR models was initially restricted to data from the pre-unification period in

---

[6]The trend is defined by means of a Hodrick-Prescott filter of the actual GDP series (see Hodrick and Prescott, 1980). Alternative estimation methods, based on production function analysis, produced similar estimates.

[7]For more details, see Sims (1980) and Todd (1991).

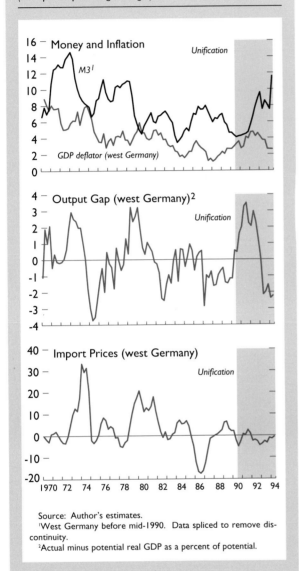

Chart 5-2. Inflation, Money, Output Gap, and Import Prices
(Four-quarter percentage changes)

Money and Inflation
Unification
M3[1]
GDP deflator (west Germany)

Output Gap (west Germany)[2]
Unification

Import Prices (west Germany)
Unification

Source: Author's estimates.
[1]West Germany before mid-1990. Data spliced to remove discontinuity.
[2]Actual minus potential real GDP as a percent of potential.

import prices, which incorporate both a potential endogenous outlet for the external transmission of monetary policy (the exchange rate) and an exogenous cost push element (world commodity prices). Import prices, the GDP deflator, and money were expressed as the four-quarter change in the logarithm of each series—the inflation rate over the course of four quarters—in order to turn these variables into stationary time series.[9] On the basis of likelihood ratio tests for higher-order terms, a maximum lag length of five was selected for the VAR models.

The analysis found evidence that all the chosen variables provide some information about inflation developments (Table 5-2). In general, the results suggest that money is a fairly robust indicator of future inflation, explaining anywhere between 27 percent and 48 percent of the error variance of inflation after five years. Nevertheless, the other variables can explain a large proportion of the remaining variance and generally provide useful independent information on future inflation.

On its own, money growth is capable of explaining some 37 percent of the error variance of inflation after five years (Table 5-2, Model 1). This simple model also confirms that causality runs from money to prices (in the sense that lagged values of money are significant determinants of inflation). The peak impact of a shock to money growth occurs after two to three years—a result in tune with the earlier visual impression in Chart 5-2.

The proportion of the error variance explained by money rises to nearly one half (Models 2 and 3) if the two nonmonetary variables—the output gap and import price inflation—are included. At the same time, the nonmonetary variables considerably reduce the forecast variance attributed in the Table to lagged inflation.[10] The importance of the output gap appears to be particularly pronounced in the short run, and after two years it explains about one third of the forecast error variance of inflation.

Analysis also confirms that the yield spread variable contains independent information that augments the overall explanatory power of the VAR models.[11] At the same time, there is some evidence that the yield spread is a useful substitute for the output gap, which would be consistent with the results

order to avoid issues of data splicing. In explaining inflation in the VAR models, the following variables were included: broad money growth and the spread between ten-year government bond yields and three-month money market rates (which capture domestic monetary conditions);[8] the output gap, defined as the ratio of real GDP to its trend value; and

---

[8]Initial estimates also examined the predictive value of equity prices. However, little significance could be found for this variable, and so the results are not reported here.

---

[9]Because statistical tests suggested that the levels of all variables, including interest rates, were integrated of order unity, there would be a risk of spurious regression results if the data were not differenced.

[10]Block exclusion tests—analogous to F-tests in a single regression but extended to the VAR system—confirm that the output gap and import price inflation provide additional explanatory power for inflation over and above that provided by money growth alone.

[11]This result is consistent with Davis and Henry (1994).

Table 5-2. Contribution to Forecast Error Variance of Inflation: Estimation Sample, 1971:3–1989:4
(In percent of total)

	Money Growth	Yield Spread	Import Price Inflation	Output Gap	Lagged Inflation
Model 1					
After two years	5.8	...	...	...	94.2
After five years	36.8	...	...	...	63.2
Model 2					
After two years	13.1	...	...	31.7	55.2
After five years	48.0	...	...	19.8	32.2
Model 3					
After two years	20.2	...	7.8	36.5	35.8
After five years	46.0	...	14.4	22.2	17.5
Model 4					
After two years	...	12.7	6.7	35.5	45.1
After five years	...	13.5	5.0	41.9	39.5
Model 5					
After two years	37.2	17.4	2.9	...	42.6
After five years	43.0	22.2	7.9	...	26.9
Model 6a[1]					
After two years	26.6	14.5	4.4	21.7	32.7
After five years	34.5	25.9	5.5	15.9	18.2
Model 6b[1]					
After two years	31.5	9.7	4.4	21.7	32.7
After five years	27.0	33.4	5.5	15.9	18.2

Source: IMF staff estimates.

[1]The orthoganalization process needed to decompose the error variance is not independent of the ordering of the variables (Sims, 1980). In model 6a, the ordering runs money growth, spread, import price inflation, gap, price inflation. In model 6b, the order of the money and spread variables are reversed. In the other models, changes in ordering had little effect on the results.

in Hu (1993) that suggest yield spreads are useful predictors of output developments. For example, in the most general model (Model 6 in Table 5-2), the inclusion of the yield spread renders the output gap variable jointly insignificant for the VAR as a whole, even though lags of the output gap are jointly quite significant in the inflation equation. In addition, there is a degree of symmetry between the results for Models 3 and 5 in Table 5-2 in which the output gap and yield spread variables appear, respectively, on their own. In general, however, the yield spread does not appear by itself to have been a good substitute for money as an indicator for future inflation (compare Models 3 and 4).

Additional information in interpreting the results is provided by an examination of the impulse responses of the VAR systems to different shocks. In the most general model, where all four monetary and nonmonetary variables are included along with inflation, a shock to money growth has a fairly immediate, but temporary, impact on the output gap and a more drawn out impact on price inflation. The latter effect gradually builds up to a peak toward the end of two years (Chart 5-3). By contrast, a positive shock to the yield spread, which might be interpreted as a lowering of short-term interest rates, has a delayed impact on output, which begins to rise significantly after a period of 18 months to 2 years.[12] While inflation reacts perversely in the short term, it is significantly higher in the medium term (Chart 5-3, middle panel). Finally, a shock to import price inflation (which could reflect unanticipated currency depreciation) appears to have a rather small impact on inflation, largely because it leads to a contraction of monetary growth—perhaps reflecting the typical policy response in the past—and the opening up of an output gap.

---

[12]This interpretation of shocks to the yield curve would be consistent with historical experience: most of the variance in the spread variable can be accounted for by variance in short-term rates as opposed to variance in bond yields.

Chart 5-3. Impulse Responses: Estimated 1970–89
(In percent)

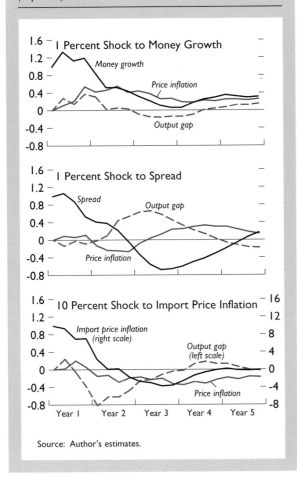

Source: Author's estimates.

Extending the Estimation After Unification

Estimates of the VAR models incorporating data from the postunification period (1990–93) indicate a smaller role for financial variables—both money and yield spreads—in explaining inflation and a significantly greater role for the output gap (Table 5-3).[13] This would be in keeping with the earlier observation that the most recent inflationary episode was not preceded by a significant upsurge in monetary growth. The result is particularly strong if united German estimates of real GDP and the GDP deflator are used: the higher inflation rate in the unified economy, against a background of much weaker

output growth, was even more at odds with the relatively benign earlier expansion of the money stock. Of course, the fall in output in east Germany and rise in price level after unification was more of a one-off adjustment, suggesting that underlying economic developments may, for the time being, be more reasonably measured by west German indicators.

Monetary Conditions Index

The previous section suggests that other financial variables, in principle, could augment or even substitute for money as an indicator of future inflation. In this section, a monetary conditions index, like the one used as an operational target for monetary policy in Canada, is constructed and its ability as an inflation indicator is compared to that of M3.

Constructing the MCI

The MCI described in Freedman (1994) is constructed as a weighted average of changes in short-term interest rates and the effective exchange rate. The two components can be expressed in either real or nominal terms, with the choice of weights based on the relative impact of each component on either real demand or prices over a six- to eight-quarter horizon. In principle, Freedman indicates a preference for a weighting of real rates based on their individual effects on real demand because this largely determines the output gap and hence inflationary pressures. In Canada's case, empirical evidence suggests a three-to-one weighting: a 1 percentage point increase in real interest rates is assumed to have the same impact on demand as a 3 percent appreciation of the real effective exchange rate. In practice, Freedman points out, the nominal- and real-based MCIs are highly collinear, and so the nominal and real MCIs provide comparable information.

A similar index was constructed for Germany. Based on simulations of a simplified model of output and inflation, a three-to-one weighting also appeared broadly appropriate—although the results were not oversensitive to different weighting choices.[14] The precise formula was as follows:

$$MCI = -(RR - RR_{85}) - 1/3(RER/RER_{85} - 1)100 \qquad (2)$$

where *RR* represents real three-month money market rates, *RER* the real effective exchange rate, and the subscript 85 refers to the level in the first quarter of 1985. It should be noted that the choice of the latter

---

[13]See the Appendix at the end of this chapter for data splicing assumptions. A dummy variable was included to allow for a potential break in behavior after the end of 1989 or to compensate for inappropriate splicing assumptions.

[14]As in the VAR simulations, interest rates influence inflation in the model through their impact on the output gap; exchange rate changes have a more direct impact on inflation.

Table 5-3. Contribution to Forecast Error Variance of Inflation: Estimation Sample, 1971:3–1993:4[1]
(In percent of total)

	Money Growth	Yield Spread	Import Price Inflation	Output Gap	Lagged Inflation
Model 1					
After two years	4.3	...	...	...	95.7
After five years	28.6	...	...	...	71.4
Model 2					
After two years	8.8	...	...	36.0	55.2
After five years	29.2	...	...	29.1	41.7
Model 3					
After two years	17.8	...	7.5	41.2	33.5
After five years	42.3	...	7.4	29.9	20.5
Model 4					
After two years	...	11.0	10.8	36.0	42.2
After five years	...	9.3	13.0	36.2	41.5
Model 5					
After two years	25.7	16.6	6.6	...	51.1
After five years	39.8	17.1	5.6	...	37.6
Model 6a[2]					
After two years	22.7	8.9	5.6	32.6	30.2
After five years	32.6	15.2	4.3	26.0	22.0
Model 6b[2]					
After two years	24.7	6.8	5.6	32.6	30.2
After five years	29.4	18.4	4.2	26.0	22.0

Source: IMF staff estimates.

[1]Data for inflation and the output gap refer to west Germany only.

[2]The orthoganalization process needed to decompose the error variance is not independent of the ordering of the variables (Sims, 1980). In model 6a, the ordering runs money growth, spread, import price inflation, gap, price inflation. In model 6b, the order of the money and spread variables are reversed. In the other models, changes in ordering had little effect on the results.

period as a benchmark is arbitrary so that no significance can be attributed to the level of the MCI. However, an increase in its value should generally reflect a loosening of monetary conditions, and vice versa for a decrease.

Up to unification, the MCI had a strong positive correlation with inflation two to three years ahead. The correlation coefficient is almost as high in magnitude as that between inflation and lagged money growth (Table 5-4).[15] However, for both money and the MCI, the correlation is very weak in the postunification period, suggesting that neither indicator would have predicted developments in inflation around the turn of the decade very well (Chart 5-4).

This is perhaps not surprising given the unprecedented nature of the demand shock to the west German economy brought on by unification. The MCI, for example, was signaling (largely on the basis of the strong real appreciation of the deutsche mark in the second half of the 1980s) that monetary conditions had been tightening for some time before unification.[16] However, it was not until after 1992 that inflation stabilized and then began to head downward. But it was also the case that, as discussed above, the rise in inflation in the late 1980s and early 1990s was not preceded by a pickup in monetary growth. Furthermore, the pickup in monetary growth from the end of 1991 onward would, on the basis of past experience, have been suggesting that inflation

[15]As in the case of Canada, the properties of the MCI were similar regardless of whether it was expressed in nominal or real terms. Nor does it make much difference (as reported in Table 5-4) whether real interest rates are defined using forward or backward measures of inflation expectations.

[16]The real exchange rate measure is based on relative normalized unit labor costs in manufacturing. As pointed out in Chapter II, this indicator may have exaggerated the implied loss of competitiveness.

Table 5-4. Inflation Correlation Coefficients

	1973–89	1973–93
MCI backward-looking price expectations		
Lagged 8	0.49	0.35
Lagged 10	0.63	0.45
Lagged 12	0.66	0.49
MCI forward-looking price expectations		
Lagged 8	0.53	0.39
Lagged 10	0.65	0.49
Lagged 12	0.63	0.50
M3 growth		
Lagged 8	0.74	0.64
Lagged 10	0.69	0.62
Lagged 12	0.64	0.59

Source: IMF staff estimates.

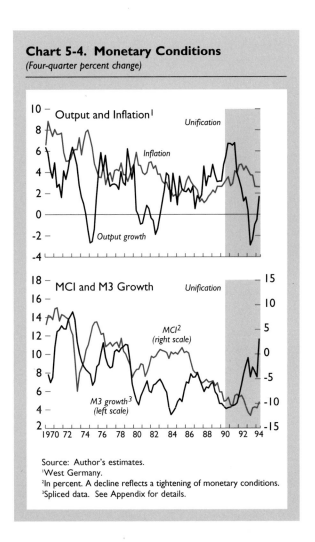

Chart 5-4. Monetary Conditions
(Four-quarter percent change)

Source: Author's estimates.
[1] West Germany.
[2] In percent. A decline reflects a tightening of monetary conditions.
[3] Spliced data. See Appendix for details.

should perhaps have begun to accelerate in 1993 and early 1994. The opposite occurred.

Implications for Recent Monetary Policy

The MCI and M3 growth provide different evaluations of German monetary conditions in the past two to three years. The early revival of money growth, dating from the end of 1991, would have suggested a significant and ongoing loosening of monetary conditions. By contrast, the MCI would have suggested that monetary conditions continued to tighten until 1993. Even in 1993, the MCI only pointed to a modest easing of monetary conditions because the effects on real interest rates of declines in short-term interest rates were offset to some extent by falling inflation, while at the same time some further appreciation of the exchange rate took place. This interpretation of monetary conditions would support the decision to cut official short-term interest rates significantly during 1993—and to continue doing so in the first half of 1994 despite the substantial overshooting of the monetary target. The decision is further validated by the sharp slowdown in M3 growth in the second half of 1994, which helped to reduce inconsistencies between the two indicators of monetary conditions.

Conclusions

On average in the past, a monetary conditions index based on interest and exchange rates would

probably have provided a useful early warning of future inflation. However, as was the case with M3, the MCI would not have been a particularly reliable predictor of inflation in the early postunification period. More recently, as M3 growth continued to exceed its target, the MCI signaled tight monetary conditions, at least until 1993, when they only began to ease gradually. This tends to support the view that concerns about a revival in inflation in the next few years are not warranted—a view corroborated by the subsequent slowdown in monetary growth in the second half of 1994.

Appendix: Data Splicing Assumptions

Time-series analysis of the postunification period requires the splicing of key data series in order to remove discontinuities associated with the enlargement of the economic area. For nominal and real GDP data, quarterly estimates for united Germany

Chart 5-A1. Inflation and Real GDP
(Four-quarter percent change)

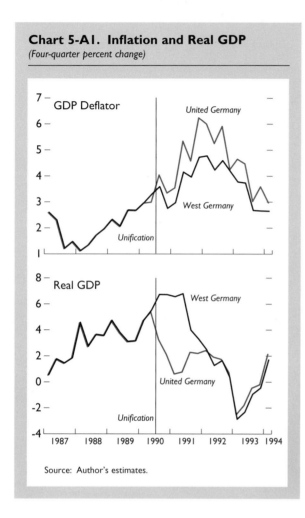

Source: Author's estimates.

Chart 5-A2. M3 Velocity[1]

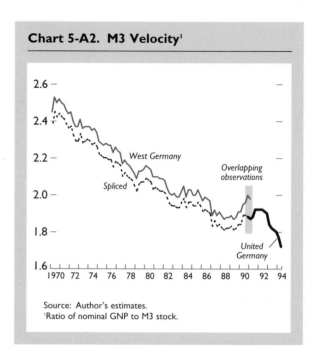

Source: Author's estimates.
[1]Ratio of nominal GNP to M3 stock.

money growth was the same in the eastern and western Länder in the third quarter of 1990.[17]

The data indicate that money velocity in the united economy during the second half of 1990 was below that in the western Länder. This might reflect, in part, the lack of nonmonetary financial investment opportunities in the former German Democratic Republic (Chart 5-A2). According to the overlapping data for the second half of 1990, the velocity of money in the united economy was as much as 6 percent lower than in the western Länder alone. However, on the basis of the splicing assumptions, the discrepancy would have been only 3 percent prior to monetary union in mid-1990.

References

Cassard, Marcel, Timothy Lane, and Paul Masson, "ERM Money Supplies and the Transition to EMU," IMF Working Paper No. 94/1 (Washington: International Monetary Fund, 1994).

Davis, E.P., and S.G.B. Henry, "The Use of Financial Spreads as Indicator Variables: Evidence for the United Kingdom. and Germany," *Staff Papers*, International Monetary Fund, Vol. 41 (September 1994), pp. 517–25.

Deutsche Bundesbank, *Monthly Report* (January 1994).

Engle, Robert F., and C.W.J. Granger, "Co-Integration and Error Correction: Representation, Estimation, and

were available from DIW from the beginning of 1990. These were spliced with earlier estimates for west Germany on the assumption that the growth rate in the first quarter of 1990 was the same in both the old and new Länder. As a result, and given the initial sharp fall in output in east Germany, real GDP growth in the unified economy is estimated to have been considerably weaker in 1990–91 than in the western Länder alone (Chart 5-A1), while inflation would have been somewhat higher because of price adjustment in the east. Thereafter, the revival of the east German economy would have had a small offsetting effect on the recession in the west.

Money stock data for the unified economy have been published on a consistent basis since the beginning of 1991, although a separate east-west monetary survey also exists for the second half of 1990. On the basis of the overlapping observations, the unified German money stock was estimated for the last two quarters of 1990 and spliced with earlier data for west Germany on the assumption that

---

[17]Some partial support for this assumption is provided by the one overlapping observation (end-June) for the second quarter of 1990. The ratio of east-west money stocks was almost exactly the same in June 1990 as in the third quarter of 1990.

Testing," *Econometrica*, Vol. 55 (March 1987), pp. 251–76.

Freedman, Charles, "The Use of Indicators and of the Monetary Conditions Index in Canada," in *Frameworks for Monetary Stability: Policy Issues and Country Experiences* (Washington: International Monetary Fund, 1994).

Hodrick, Robert, and Edward C. Prescott, "Post-War U.S. Business Cycles: An Empirical Investigation" (unpublished; Pittsburgh: Carnegie-Mellon University, 1980).

Hu, Zuliu, "The Yield Curve and Real Activity," *Staff Papers*, International Monetary Fund, Vol. 40 (December 1993), pp. 781–806.

Schinasi, Gary, "Asset Prices, Monetary Policy, and the Business Cycle," IMF Paper on Policy Analysis and Assessment No. 94/6 (Washington: International Monetary Fund, 1994).

Sims, Christopher A., "Macroeconomics and Reality," *Econometrica*, Vol. 48 (January 1980), pp. 1–48.

Todd, Richard M., "Vector Autoregression Evidence on Monetarism: Another Look at the Robustness Debate," *Federal Reserve Bank of Minneapolis Quarterly Review* (Spring 1991), pp. 19–37.

von Hagen, Jürgen, "Monetary Union, Money Demand, and Money Supply: A Review of German Monetary Union," *European Economic Review*, Vol. 37 (1993).

VI Prospects for Self-Sustaining Growth in Eastern Germany

Karl Habermeier

Considerable progress has been made in restructuring the economy of eastern Germany. The system of economic planning in existence at the time of economic and monetary union in mid-1990 has been replaced by a social market economy on the west German model. Most west German laws and institutions were extended to eastern Germany at the time of unification, and there has been further institutional convergence since then. Privatization has proceeded quickly; by the end of 1994, virtually all of the former state-owned enterprises had been transferred to private ownership. The transformation has been more profound and complete than in any other country in transition in central and eastern Europe. Eastern Germany now possesses a stable political and legal framework, a substantial private enterprise sector, and a comprehensive social safety net.

These achievements have not been without cost: transfer payments from west Germany increased to about 5 percent of total German GDP by 1993 (Table 6-1). The restructuring process has also been accompanied by a large decline in measured production and a massive shakeout of labor.[1] However, the downturn in production bottomed out in 1991, and gross domestic product has been increasing ever since at annual rates of between 5 and 10 percent (Table 6-2).

Nonetheless, the question remains whether growth in east Germany can be sustained. There has been concern that the rapid increase in east German wages, which are now far higher than warranted by productivity, could hamper private investment. Moreover, the increase in output since 1991 has been concentrated in nontraded activities, such as construction and retail trade, which may have been stimulated by growing transfers from west Germany. Manufacturing output and exports of goods, on the other hand, have remained relatively weak, although signs of a stronger upswing were emerging in early 1994.

Inadequate economic growth in east Germany could make the region even more reliant on transfer payments and have serious repercussions for the public finances and macroeconomic performance of Germany as a whole. This chapter reviews in more detail some of the factors affecting prospects for an upswing in east Germany, including institutional arrangements, investment, and conditions in the labor market. On the basis of this analysis, an attempt is made to incorporate the most salient features into a quantitative framework for assessing potential growth. The simulations suggest that the prospects for growth are relatively good but that employment will continue to decline unless supported by policy intervention.

Determinants of Growth

Investment

The standard neoclassical view of economic growth is that in the very long run, when the economy has reached a steady state, the growth rate of per capita income depends on the rate of technological innovation. During the transition to the steady state, when the economy is undergoing a process of capital deepening, the growth rate also depends on the rate at which capital is accumulated.

The east German economy at the time of unification was far from a steady state. The inherited capital stock was of little value in a market economy, and technology lagged behind the west by perhaps two decades. Productivity and per capita incomes were substantially lower than in west Germany.

Neoclassical theory implies that economic growth in east Germany will be driven for a considerable time by capital accumulation. The speed of this process, and hence the rate of economic growth, will depend largely on the amount of new productive investment. The propensity of private enterprises to invest depends, in turn, on a multiplicity of factors affecting the rate of return on capital. These include the degree of political stability, the efficiency and honesty of public administration, the condition of

---

[1]The size of the drop has most likely been exaggerated. Estimates of pre-unification gross domestic product are too high in that they do not adequately reflect differences in quality between western and eastern products.

Table 6-1. Public Transfers to Eastern Germany
(In billions of deutsche mark)

	1991[1]	1992[1]	1993[2]	1994[2]
Federal Government[3]	75	89	117	119
West German Länder governments and local authorities[4]	5	5	10	14
"German Unity" Fund	31	24	15	5
EC budget	4	5	5	6
Federal Labor Office[5]	25	24	18	18
Statutory pension insurance funds	—	5	12	12
Gross transfers, total[6]	140	152	177	174
less: Receipts of the Federal Government in eastern Germany[7]	33	35	39	42
Net transfers, total	107	117	138	132

Source: Deutsche Bundesbank, *Monthly Report* (September 1993).
[1] Partly estimated.
[2] Estimated.
[3] Including financial assistance to the Federal Labor Office.
[4] Including the waiver of turnover tax revenue as a result of the population-based distribution of this tax.
[5] Corresponds to the share of the deficit incurred in eastern Germany, which is being financed by west German contribution payments.
[6] Excluding tax concessions, interest-subsidized loans, and interest payments due to unification.
[7] Tax revenue and administrative reports.

the infrastructure, the availability of a labor force that is technically skilled and diligent, and the level of wages.

An important objective of economic policy in the region, therefore, has been to create an environment conducive to private investment. A considerable effort has been devoted to rebuilding east Germany's public infrastructure, especially in the critical fields of transportation and telecommunications. Moreover, the Government has made available generous assistance to potential investors in the region, including special tax allowances, accelerated depreciation, and subsidized credit. Several laws were passed to ensure that the property rights of investors took precedence over the restitution claims of former owners. Finally, the Treuhand has required buyers of its enterprises to make a contractual commitment to a specified volume of investment.[2]

These policies appear to have met with some success, although it is difficult to know how investment would have performed in their absence. There has been a marked increase in gross fixed investment, from less than 20 percent of GDP in 1990 to around 50 percent of GDP in 1993 (Table 6-2). There has also been a shift in the perceptions of investors. Early surveys showed that bottlenecks in public ad-

ministration, a lack of market opportunities, uncertainty about property rights, and an inadequate transportation and telecommunications infrastructure were seen as important obstacles to investment. In more recent surveys, these concerns have moved to the background.

Wages and Employment

Instead, the high level of wages in east Germany has assumed greater prominence in the surveys on the obstacles to investment. This section examines the relationship among the level of wages, employment, and the incentive to invest.

The sharp increase in wages following unification can be attributed to a desire of labor unions to eliminate the wage differential with west Germany. The ostensible motivations for this policy were equity ("equal pay for equal work") and the desire to reduce migration to west Germany.[3] As a result, wage

[2] These commitments have been linked with a commitment to maintain a specified level of employment. See section below.

[3] The early wage negotiations in east Germany were dominated by union representatives from west Germany, who may have been eager to avoid low-wage competition from east Germany, and enterprise management was still predominantly in the hands of officials appointed by the old east German Government, who offered little resistance to union demands. In some cases, for example, in the metals industry, agreements reached a few months following unification provided for a full adjustment of wages in east Germany to west German levels within a few years. Some of the more generous agreements have since been amended.

Table 6-2. Eastern Germany: Basic Economic Indicators

	1990	1991	1992	1993
Output and employment				
Real GDP[1]	...	−18.7	7.8	5.8
Employment[1]	...	−14.9	−10.4	−3.0
Productivity[2]	...	−1.9	22.1	9.0
Investment				
Gross fixed investment[3]	28.1	44.7	48.1	49.1
Private[3]	23.2	37.7	39.7	41.3
Business[3]	15.8	29.6	30.2	30.5
Residential[3]	7.5	8.1	9.5	10.8
Public[3]	4.9	7.0	8.4	7.8
Business investment per employed person[4]	38.4	80.3	116.6	141.2
In percent of west German level	34.6	66.2	96.6	132.6
Public investment per capita[5]	6.6	9.1	14.0	15.3
In percent of west German level	75.4	97.2	141.9	160.1
Labor costs				
Marginal product of labor[6]	13.4	14.9	21.2	25.5
Average gross wage[7]	16.7	21.8	29.5	32.9
In percent of west German level	39.7	49.1	62.7	68.0
Share of labor income[8]	87.6	101.9	99.1	94.2
Labor market				
Employment (millions)	8.923	7.590	6.801	6.598
Participants in labor market programs[9]	...	2.064	1.763	1.463
In percent of employment	...	27.2	25.9	22.2
Unemployment rate[10]	2.9	10.7	14.7	14.8
West Germany	6.2	5.5	5.8	7.3

Sources: Data provided by the authorities; and IMF staff calculations.
[1] Percent changes.
[2] Real GDP per employed person, percent change.
[3] Percent of GDP.
[4] Gross business investment per employed person (in thousands of deutsche mark).
[5] Per population (in thousands of deutsche mark).
[6] Nominal GDP per employed person (multiplied by normal share of labor).
[7] Gross income from dependent employment per employee (in thousands of deutsche mark).
[8] Gross income from dependent employment as percent of national income.
[9] Retraining, job creation, short-time work, early retirement.
[10] In percent of labor force.

rates have been far out of line with productivity. Not only is the average wage rate substantially higher than the marginal product of labor but the share of labor in national income exceeds 100 percent, implying that the aggregate current profitability of the business sector is negative (Table 6-2).

Excessive wages affect both the level of output and the propensity to invest. The effect on the level of output results from the reduction in the demand for labor. Indeed, employment has declined every year since unification (Table 6-2). Although some initial decline in employment was to be expected, if only because labor force participation under central planning was artificially high, employment has continued to fall even though production bottomed out in the course of 1991.

The effect of excessive wages on the propensity to invest, and hence on the growth rate of output in the medium term, is of greater consequence. For any given level of total factor productivity, both the real wage and the real implied return on capital are determined by the capital-labor ratio. When a profit-maximizing firm increases its capital-labor ratio in response to higher wages, which in the short run can be accomplished only by cutting employment, the implied rate of return on capital declines, reducing the incentive to invest. In principle, extremely high wages could completely stifle new investment unless offsetting measures are taken.

As mentioned above, the Government has taken a number of measures to stimulate investment. In addition, direct and indirect labor subsidies are widespread in east Germany. They have helped to mitigate the adverse effect of high wages on investment and growth. Workers in special labor market programs accounted for about one fifth of total employ-

Table 6-3. Eastern Germany: Trade and Payments

	1990	1991	1992	1993
	(In billions of deutsche mark)			
Goods and nonfactor services				
Exports	35.1	46.9	52.1	54.9
Imports	91.6	199.2	246.8	261.6
Foreign balance	−56.5	−152.3	−194.7	−206.7
Balance of factor services	2.0	8.0	10.8	9.4
Balance of transfers	...	107.0	117.0	138.0
Current balance	...	−37.3	−66.9	−59.3
Implicit capital account balance	...	37.3	66.9	59.3
	(In percent of GDP)			
Goods and nonfactor services				
Exports	16.1	22.8	19.8	18.0
Imports	42.1	96.7	94.0	85.7
Foreign balance	−26.0	−73.9	−74.1	−67.7
Balance of factor services	0.9	3.9	4.1	3.1
Balance of transfers	...	51.9	44.6	45.2
Current balance	...	−18.1	−25.5	−19.4
Implicit capital account balance	...	18.1	25.5	19.4

Sources: Data supplied by the authorities; and IMF staff calculations.

ment in 1991–93.[4] Moreover, the Treuhand has required buyers of enterprises to make a commitment to maintain employment at a specified level for some years. In exchange for these commitments, the Treuhand provided a subsidy by reducing the price charged to the buyers.[5]

There is a growing recognition that these measures may not be sufficient and that wage moderation and greater wage flexibility may also be needed to forestall a further significant rise in unemployment and to enhance the incentive to invest in east Germany. Numerous enterprises have left the employers' associations, and there is evidence that many have been paying wages below the official tariff without much protest from the unions. Moreover, many labor unions have now distanced themselves from the objective of achieving wage parity with west Germany in the next few years. There has also been a somewhat greater willingness on the part of the labor unions to permit the negotiation of special wage concessions at the plant level when jobs are in jeopardy.

Composition of Demand and Output

While the adequacy of aggregate investment and labor market conditions are the most fundamental determinants of economic growth, the composition of demand and output also provides information on the likely pace of economic expansion. Aggregate demand in east Germany currently exceeds output by a wide margin, and there is a substantial trade imbalance (Table 6-3). Demand is sustained by large net transfer payments and by a substantial inflow of capital. The capital inflow partly finances private investment and partly finances the borrowing of state and local governments and the Treuhand.[6]

Put differently, east Germany's massive trade deficit is the necessary counterpart of the inflows of transfers and capital. The domestic tradable goods sector (which consists principally of manufacturing

---

[4]These programs include short-time work, job creation measures, and retraining. Recipients of special early retirement benefits are also counted as employed.

[5]Taking into account various subsidies for restructuring, debt relief, and other forms of assistance, the effective price charged to buyers of enterprises was, in many cases, zero or even negative.

[6]Public borrowing in east Germany amounted to DM 52 billion in 1993 (about 20 percent of GDP).

Table 6-4. Eastern Germany: Gross Value Added by Sector

	Percent Changes			Percent of Total			
	1991	1992	1993	1990	1991	1992	1993
Agriculture and forestry	−66.1	18.8	41.1	2.9	1.3	1.4	1.9
Industry	−34.3	14.3	11.1	41.5	35.8	37.6	39.2
Mining and energy	−13.8	−12.2	−5.0	6.9	7.8	6.3	5.6
Manufacturing	−49.1	17.2	10.6	24.4	16.3	17.5	18.2
Construction	−12.8	28.1	19.2	10.2	11.7	13.8	15.4
Total services	−13.6	5.4	3.3	55.5	62.9	61.0	59.0
Trade and transport	−36.9	−3.0	7.5	18.4	15.2	13.6	13.7
Trade	−40.4	−0.2	5.7	12.6	9.9	9.1	9.0
Transport	−29.0	−8.2	11.2	5.7	5.3	4.5	4.7
Other private services	11.3	16.7	2.7	16.3	23.7	25.5	24.5
Public sector, private households, and nonprofit organizations	−12.5	−0.5	1.3	20.9	24.0	21.9	20.8
Gross value added	−23.7	8.8	6.7	100.0	100.0	100.0	100.0

Source: Deutsches Institut für Wirtschaftsforschung.

industry) was simply unable to satisfy the surge in demand brought on by these inflows. Moreover, the east German manufacturing sector was uncompetitive. Many goods were of low quality, at least initially, and costs were, and in some cases remain, excessive.[7] Compared with 1990, the share of manufacturing in value added has fallen sharply, to less than 20 percent (Table 6-4). Although it has recovered somewhat since 1990, it remains well below the industrialized country norm. In west Germany, for example, the share of manufacturing in value added has been around 30 percent in recent years.

The decline in the share of manufacturing and other tradable items was mirrored by a marked shift in the structure of production toward nontradables, such as private services and construction; these activities have made a substantial contribution to the growth of output in east Germany in 1992 and 1993. However, there has been concern that, as transfers to east Germany stabilize, the impetus these transfers have imparted to the nontradables sector will also level off. With little further expansion in the nontradables sector, even a relatively rapid increase in the output of manufactures and other tradables

would produce only slow economic growth, given the small share of the tradables sector in overall value added. In sum, there would be a deceleration in economic growth as transfers from west Germany level off or decline.

An assessment of this observation would begin by defining the (disposable) income of the east German economy as the sum of domestic net production and net transfers. It then becomes apparent that in 1992–93, the share of income absorbed by nontradables amounted to only 54 percent, substantially below the comparable ratio for west Germany (64 percent). Hence, there is considerable room for a further expansion of the nontradables sector. The extent to which the slackening of transfer payments to east Germany is likely to constrain economic growth is taken up in the quantitative framework developed below.

Quantitative Framework

In this section, an attempt is made to quantify the interplay among several of the key variables affecting economic growth: output, investment, wages, and employment. The model is based on the neoclassical theory of capital accumulation and growth. At its core are aggregate production functions and investment equations, all of which are calibrated on the basis of the historical experience in west Germany. Labor market conditions are analyzed by deriving labor demand functions using standard marginal productivity conditions.

---

[7]In the immediate aftermath of unification, east German consumers were reluctant to purchase poorly made domestic products. Producers in east Germany have in the meantime sharply upgraded quality and are beginning to regain the confidence of consumers and to increase their market share. The collapse of trade with the countries of the former socialist bloc has added to the woes of east German manufacturing, as have the difficulties of developing new markets in western Europe and elsewhere.

Overview of the Model

Three sectors are distinguished: tradables, private nontradables, and public nontradables.[8] Output in each sector (denoted by i) is represented by a Cobb-Douglas production function and indexed by time period t:

$$Q_{ti} = A_{ti} K_{ti}^{\alpha} L_{ti}^{1-\alpha} \qquad (1)$$

where Q_{ti} is output, A_{ti} is total factor productivity, K_{ti} is capital stock, and L_{ti} is labor input. The production elasticities of the factors, denoted by α, are the same across sectors.[9] As indicated in the previous section, the overall income of the economy is the sum of output and net transfers:

$$\begin{aligned} Y_t &= Q_t + TR_t, \\ Q_t &= Q_{t,T} + Q_{t,NP} + Q_{t,NG}, \end{aligned} \qquad (2)$$

where Q_t is output, TR_t are transfers, and the subscripts T, NP, and NG refer to tradables, private nontradables, and public nontradables sectors.

The government sector is assumed to be essentially static, with value added remaining constant in real terms for most of the forecast horizon and increasing in step with value added in the other sectors in the longer run. For the sake of simplicity, the projections also assume that net transfers remain constant in real terms over the entire horizon. Moreover, the share of the nontradables sector in overall income is assumed to converge to the equilibrium share according to a partial adjustment process:

$$\begin{aligned} \sigma_{t+1} &= \sigma_t + \xi(\bar{\sigma} - \sigma_t), \\ \sigma_t &= \frac{Q_{t,NP} + Q_{t,NG}}{Y_t} \end{aligned} \qquad (3)$$

where the parameter σ is chosen to achieve the bulk of the adjustment in 20 years or so. Then, income is determined as

$$Y_t = \frac{Q_{t,T} + TR_t}{1 - \sigma_t} \qquad (4)$$

The next task is to determine output in the tradable goods sector, which requires a model of investment and the demand for labor. With this model in hand, overall income and output can be determined, as well as the distribution of factors across sectors.

Derivation of the Investment Function

The investment function is based on the solution to the profit-maximization problem of a representative firm. Profits are maximized subject to the constraint of technology (the production function) but also subject to a term representing costs associated with changes in the capital stock. The solution to this problem (see the Appendix at the end of this chapter for details) produces a formula for investment that can be recognized as a partial adjustment model:

$$K_{t+1} = zK_t + \frac{F_K(K_t, L_t, A_t) - (r_t + \gamma)}{\Psi(1 + r_t - z)}. \qquad (5)$$

In the limit, assuming r_t goes to r = constant, K_t asymptotically increases each period by a factor of z and the marginal product of capital equals $r + \gamma$, the sum of the real rate of return on capital and the rate of depreciation. It is easy to show that the parameter $z - 1$ is the steady-state growth rate of the economy: that is, the rate at which the capital-output ratio remains constant.

The investment function was calibrated on the basis of west German data (again, details may be found in the Appendix). For the purposes of the simulations, the following related, and relatively simple, form was used:

$$\frac{K_{t+1} - zK_t}{Y_t} = \alpha_0 + \alpha_1 \left[\frac{\bar{K}}{\bar{Y}} - \frac{K_t}{Y_t} \right]. \qquad (6)$$

It might be noted that calibrating the investment function on the basis of the west German experience may understate the volume of investment that can be expected in east Germany. In particular, investment in east Germany is unlikely to be constrained by the availability of domestic savings as may have been the case in west Germany in the period 1960–90. The estimates also do not take account of the large subsidies for investment available in east Germany and so may again understate the propensity to invest in east Germany.[10] On the other hand, the fact that Germany was a net exporter of savings for much of the period suggests that the savings constraint may not have been binding. In any event, it is probably safer to underestimate investment than to overestimate it.

---

[8]The tradables sector is assumed to consist of manufacturing plus transport and telecommunications. Data limitations prevent a more precise delineation, which would include some other tradable services. It is also assumed that the entire value added of the government sector is nontradable.

[9]It is straightforward to show that, provided the market wage and cost of capital faced by each sector are the same, and that the marginal conditions for profit maximization hold, the aggregate production function for the economy as a whole also has the Cobb-Douglas form. In this production function, the aggregate factors of production (capital and labor) are the sum of the factors of production employed in the individual sectors, and total factor productivity is a weighted sum of sectoral total factor productivity, where the weights are the share of labor employed in the individual sectors. Moreover, the marginal conditions for profit maximization hold for the aggregate production function.

---

[10]An attempt can be made to correct for this by changing the steady-state cost of capital r.

Table 6-5. Range of Initial Conditions in Eastern Germany

			Range		
Total factor productivity (in percent of west German level)	20.0	40.0	60.0	80.0	100.0
Capital stock (ratio to real GDP)	18.7	3.7	1.5	0.7	0.4

Calibration of the Production Functions

Before proceeding to the more complex task of calibrating the multisector model, it is worth making some observations about the overall situation. Aggregate labor productivity in east Germany, as measured by real GDP per employed person, was about 34 percent of the west German level in 1990. In terms of the Cobb-Douglas production function used here, lower labor productivity can be explained by a lower capital-labor ratio, by lower total factor productivity, or by some combination of both.[11] As there is no reliable information on the level of the capital stock in east Germany around the time of unification, it is not possible to determine both the capital-labor ratio and total factor productivity. One or the other will have to be arbitrarily set based on broad considerations of plausibility and consistency. In this connection, it should be noted that for any given level of labor productivity, there is an inverse relationship between total factor productivity and the implied capital stock. Table 6-5 illustrates this point (assuming Y/L equals 28.40, the 1990 value for east Germany).

Thus, the range of estimates for the initial capital stock varies by a factor of ten or more. Some of the more extreme estimates are easily ruled out on the basis of plausibility considerations. The well-known inefficiency of resource allocation in east Germany's planned economy and the outmoded technology widely used there make it unlikely that total factor productivity reached 100 percent, or even 80 percent of the west German level. It is also improbable that the capital-output ratio greatly exceeded comparable values in west Germany, where it ranged from about 1.4 in 1960 to 2.0 in the late 1980s. Plausible estimates would put total factor productivity in east Germany at about 50 to 70 percent of the west German level.

Of course, total factor productivity should be expected to increase quickly from this initial level, eventually converging to the west German standard. Substantially improved technology has begun to be employed, and there has been a large influx of west German specialists in management, marketing, and finance. In the manufacturing sector, there are many examples of new facilities established in east Germany that incorporate the most advanced technology. Indeed, most of these enterprises are more productive than the average west German facility. By contrast, in the nontradables sector, less efficient enterprises may be able to persist for a considerably longer period of time.

In the final analysis, total factor productivity in the initial year (1990) in both the tradables sector and the private nontradables sector was set at 60 percent of the west German level. By 1994, total factor productivity in the severely diminished tradable goods sector is assumed to reach 77 percent of the west German level, and it increases to 100 percent of the west German level over the next 15 years. In the larger nontradables sector, it increases to 70 percent in 1994 and then rises much more gradually, not reaching 100 percent of the west German level until 20 years later. Although these assumptions are somewhat arbitrary, there is no alternative to making judgments of this kind if the objective is to provide a quantitative assessment of the growth prospects in east Germany.

Modeling the Labor Market

The production functions, combined with estimates of the initial level of the capital stock, allow for the derivation of sectoral labor demand functions that take the following form:

$$L_{ti} = [(1 - \alpha) A_{ti} K_{ti}^{\alpha} w_{ti}^{-1}]^{1/\alpha}, \tag{7}$$

where w_{ti} is the real wage.[12] As mentioned earlier, the level of employment currently seen in east Germany is higher than would be consistent with this

---

[11]Part of the shortfall could also be explained by differences in the production elasticities of capital and labor. More generally, the form of the production function could have been entirely different. A full evaluation of these possibilities is beyond the scope of this study.

[12]This wage is defined as nominal gross wages per employed person divided by the output deflator.

Table 6-6. Eastern Germany: Growth Scenario

	1994	1995	1996	1997	1998	1999
Real GDP	8.2	8.4	8.8	8.6	8.7	8.9
Tradables	9.2	9.0	10.6	11.0	11.6	12.3
Nontradables	8.0	8.3	8.4	8.0	8.0	8.0
Percentage shares in GDP						
Tradables	20.2	20.3	20.6	21.1	21.6	22.3
Nontradables	79.8	79.7	79.4	78.9	78.4	77.7
Employment	−1.8	−0.3	−0.1	0.1	0.3	0.6
Labor market gap[1]	46.2	42.0	37.6	33.0	28.1	22.9
Real wage	3.7	2.4	2.8	3.0	3.0	3.0
Percent of west	73.4	74.9	75.3	75.6	75.9	76.3
Gross investment[2]	24.2	23.1	22.2	21.5	20.9	20.4
West Germany	13.5	13.7	13.9	14.1	14.2	14.4

Source: IMF staff calculations.
[1]In percent of employment.
[2]Nonresidential investment (in percent of GDP).

labor demand function; this reflects the operation of various labor market support schemes. For the purposes of the simulation, it is assumed that these support schemes will continue to be phased out during the 1990s. In the model, this is represented by a progressive narrowing of the gap between notional labor demand, given the exogenously determined path of wage adjustment, and the actual level of employment.

Once the labor market gap has been fully eliminated, the pace of wage adjustment is set so as to allow for convergence of the unemployment rate to the NAIRU (assumed to be 10 percent) within a number of years.[13] After the NAIRU has been reached, wages are determined endogenously to keep the unemployment rate constant.

Simulation Results and Cautionary Notes

The principal result is that the outlook for self-sustaining growth in eastern Germany seems to be rather good, with growth rates of between 8 and 9 percent for the remainder of this decade (Table 6-6). These growth rates are sustained by investment that is considerably higher than in west Germany and by the gradual convergence of total factor productivity to the west German level. The tradable goods sector, which contracted sharply following unification, is

expected to grow more rapidly than the nontradable sector, and there is consequently a gradual increase in the share of tradable goods production in the economy. Beyond the turn of the century, the rate of economic expansion is projected to decrease toward its steady-state value, with GDP growth averaging about 6 percent in 2000–09 and 3 percent in 2010–19.

The outlook for the labor market is considerably less favorable and fraught with risks, which could have adverse repercussions for growth. Wages are much higher than compatible with full employment.[14] A pronounced recovery in employment is therefore not likely to occur until after the turn of the century, and an equilibrium in the labor market will not be reached before 2005.[15]

An indicator of pressure in the labor market is the "gap" shown in Table 6-6. This is the difference between notional labor demand (at the exogenously determined level of wages) and actual employment.[16] This measure shows that employment will

---

[13]As will be seen below in the discussion of the quantitative results, the labor market gap will continue to exist for at least the remainder of this decade.

[14]Gross wages per employed person increase from 70 percent of the west German level in 1993 to 76 percent by 1999. The growth of real gross wages per employed person in west Germany is assumed to average 2½ percent a year in 1996–99, following a slight decline in 1993–94.

[15]Labor market equilibrium is defined as a measured unemployment rate equal to the NAIRU, without a need for policies to maintain employment.

[16]This estimate is subject to a large margin of error. If the level of total factor productivity in the nontradable sector were to increase to 85 percent of the west German level by 1999 (instead of 76 percent in the baseline and the same level as in the tradable goods sector), the share of employment not warranted by wages and productivity could decline to less than 15 percent by 1999.

for some years remain substantially higher than warranted by productivity and wages. In these circumstances, the scenario assumes that a further rapid contraction of employment will be forestalled by active labor market support measures and by the employment guarantees obtained from buyers of enterprises by the Treuhand. Moreover, there are important adjustment costs to reducing the labor force. For example, German labor law makes provision for large severance payments. These adjustment costs, which have not been formally represented in the model, combined with the expectation that the gap between wages and productivity will narrow, may induce employers to maintain employment at a higher level than desirable from a purely short-term perspective. Such calculations, however, are subject to serious risks. If enterprises come to realize that they have overestimated the potential markets for east German products or the pace of productivity improvements, they may decide that a further round of layoffs is indicated. This outcome would dampen the prospects for growth during the period when the layoffs occur.

These risks could be substantially reduced and labor market performance improved if real wages in east Germany were frozen at their 1994 level until 1998. The adoption of this policy by the labor unions would reverse, to some extent, the excessive convergence of east German wages toward west German levels that has taken place since 1990. As a result, the labor market gap would virtually vanish by 1999, with notional labor demand about 1½ million (20 percent of labor force) higher than in the baseline scenario.

The results presented above need to be interpreted with considerable caution, as they are highly sensitive to the assumptions made about production, investment, and labor demand. First, although the volume of investment that has taken place in east Germany is high by any standard, its productivity may be rather different from that assumed in the model. For example, if total factor productivity in the tradables sector reached 100 percent of the west German level in another 5 years rather than in 15 years, the growth rate for the overall economy would be well over 10 percent during the second half of the 1990s.

Second, even if investment were as productive as assumed, the east German manufacturing sector may not be able to gain market share as quickly as the model implies. New entrants and local ventures, in particular, may be at a significant disadvantage compared with established producers in other industrial countries, in that they lack market power, access to proprietary technologies, and an established customer base. It should be remembered, though, that many production facilities in east Germany were purchased or newly established by large and well-capitalized multinational enterprises.

Third, it is also possible that deteriorating conditions in the labor market could prompt measures to sustain employment by expanding the "secondary" labor market—that is, through various job creation schemes. To the extent that these activities discourage work effort or compete with the private sector, they could prove to be an obstacle to profitable private investment and economic growth.

Despite these possible concerns, the growth rates projected by the model are not too high compared with what has been observed in many of the newly industrialized countries of Asia and with Germany's own economic recovery after the war.[17] Although there are risks, especially those stemming from excessively high wages, there is also a possibility that total factor productivity in manufacturing could improve more quickly than anticipated. If the growth rates envisaged in the baseline scenario are achieved, the economic restructuring of east Germany could be considered a success.

Appendix: Derivation and Estimation of Investment Function

Behavioral relationships are derived from the profit-maximization problem of the representative firm

$$\max_{\{K_t, L_t, D_t\}} \sum_{t=0}^{\infty} \delta_t \, [F(K_t, L_t, A_t) - (K_{t+1} - K_t) - \gamma K_t - g(K_{t+1}, K_t) - w_t L_t - r_t D_t + (D_{t+1} - D_t)],$$

where δ_t is the discount factor, w_t is the real wage, γ is the depreciation rate, r_t is the implied real rate of return (inclusive of taxes and subsidies) on enterprise debt (or equity) D_t, and the function $g(.)$ represents an adjustment cost to capital formation.[18]

The Euler equations for this problem are the following (subscripts denote partial derivatives):

$$F_L(K_t, L_t, A_t) = w_t,$$

$$\delta_{t-1} = (1 + r_t)\delta_t,$$

$$\delta_t \, [F_K(K_t, L_t, A_t) + (1 - \gamma)K_t - g_2(K_{t+1}, K_t)] - \delta_{t-1}[1 + g_1(K_t, K_{t-1})] = 0.$$

---

[17]During the 1950s, the growth of real GDP in west Germany averaged 8 percent a year, while manufacturing output increased at an annual rate of more than 10 percent.

[18]Output Q_t is a function of the capital stock K_t, labor input L_t, and the level of total factor productivity A_t (which represents exogenous technological change):

$$Q_t = F(K_t, L_t, A_t).$$

As usual, it is assumed that the production function is homogenous of degree one in capital and labor.

Note that in the absence of the adjustment cost terms, the last equation reduces to the well-known marginal condition

$$F_K(K_t, L_t, A_t) = r_t + \gamma.$$

In other words, without an adjustment cost or other similar constraint on the speed of capital formation, the capital stock would instantaneously jump to its steady-state level.

Assuming that the adjustment cost function is quadratic,

$$g(K_{t+1}, K_t) = \frac{\psi}{2}(K_{t+1} - K_t)^2,$$

the difference equation for the capital stock may be written in the form shown in the body of the chapter.

In applying the investment equation, it will also be assumed that the production function takes the Cobb-Douglas form and that total factor productivity is given by an exogenous trend ($A_t = Ab^t$):

$$Q_t = Ab^t K_t^{\alpha} L_t^{1-\alpha}.$$

Then, it may be shown that the steady-state growth factor is given by

$$z = b^{\frac{1}{1-\alpha}} n,$$

where n is the steady-state growth rate of labor input.

The production function can be estimated in the usual way, using west German data. First, the parameter α is equal to the share of labor. Taking the average of the ratio of gross income from dependent employment to GDP over the period 1960–90 yields $1 - \alpha = 0.57$, so $\alpha = 0.43$. Second, total factor productivity (TFP) was derived as a residual by removing the contributions of capital and labor to output:

$$\ln A_t = \ln Y_t - \alpha \ln K_t - (1 - \alpha) \ln L_t.$$

A linear trend was fitted to the resulting series (see Chart 6-A1),

$$\ln A_t = 0.00989\, t - 17.4292, \quad R^2 = 0.9481,$$
$$\quad\quad\;\; (24.1829) \quad (21.5570)$$

implying a long-term increase in TFP of about 1 percent a year. Similar results were obtained by adjusting TFP using the Hodrick-Prescott filter and taking percentage changes, although this method of adjustment reveals that there were long swings in the growth rate of TFP, with a sharp decline from the late 1960s to the early 1980s and then an increase that lasted until German unification in 1990. Assuming that total factor productivity grows by 1 percent

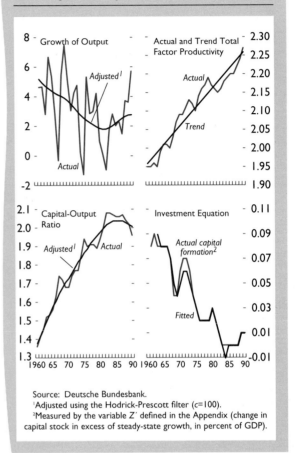

Chart 6-A1. West Germany: Output, Productivity, and Capital

Source: Deutsche Bundesbank.
[1]Adjusted using the Hodrick-Prescott filter (c=100).
[2]Measured by the variable Z' defined in the Appendix (change in capital stock in excess of steady-state growth, in percent of GDP).

(or slightly more) and employment by 0.3 percent, this would be consistent with a steady-state growth rate of about 2 percent.[19]

Assuming a Cobb-Douglas production function and a quadratic adjustment cost function, the difference equation for the capital stock is

$$K_{t+1} = z K_t + \frac{\alpha \dfrac{Y_t}{K_t} - (r_t + \gamma)}{\psi(1 + r_t - z)}.$$

The equation and the parameter estimates (using data for 1960 to 1990) are

$$K_t = \beta_1 K_{t-1} + \beta_2 \frac{Y_{t-1}}{K_{t-1}} \beta_3 + e_t,$$

---

[19]The growth of the labor force and employment in west Germany since the mid-1980s has been substantially faster (about ¾ percent a year, on average), reflecting high immigration. Whether immigration and labor force growth will continue at this rate over the longer term is an open question. If it did, the steady-state growth rate would be closer to 2½ percent.

$\beta_1 = 0.99555$ (86.3423)
$\beta_2 = 71.7808$ (0.42747)
$\beta_3 = 93.1979$ (0.71974)

$R^2 = 0.9997$, $DW = 0.4956$

This equation has a number of problems. In addition to strong serial correlation in the residuals, severe multicollinearity is present, resulting in unstable parameter estimates when estimated over different time periods. In particular, the estimated steady-state growth rate of capital, 1 percent, is inconsistent with what was derived from the information about the share of labor and the growth of total factor productivity.

The equation was hence reestimated, imposing the earlier estimate of 2.1 percent for the steady-state growth rate and using $Z_t = K_t - 1.021K_{t-1}$ as the dependent variable. This yielded $R^2 = 0.6850$ and highly significant estimates for β_2 and β_3. With the Durbin-Watson statistic equal to 0.2984, serial correlation in the residuals remained a problem.

Two approaches were taken to address the serial correlation. The first was simply to adjust the preceding equation using Cochrane-Orcutt. The second was to use a more general dynamic specification that includes lagged values of the dependent variable. The first method gave parameter estimates $\beta_2 = 995.466$ (7.33627) and $\beta_3 = -472.383$ (6.97133), with $R^2 = 0.9585$. These estimates can be used to derive a value for ψ and for the steady-state capital-output ratio. In particular, it is known that

$$\beta_1 = z,$$

$$\beta_2 = \frac{\alpha}{\psi(1 + r - z)},$$

$$\beta_3 = \frac{r + \gamma}{\psi(1 + r - z)},$$

and that $\alpha = 0.43$. An estimate of γ equals 0.05 was obtained from data on the capital stock and depreciation. Solving the equations yields $r = 0.154$ and $\psi =$ 0.00325, implying that K/Y is 2.11 in the steady state.[20] These results need to be treated with some caution, as the calculation assumes that long-term r is exogenous, constant, and inferable from past investment behavior. Rather, it is likely that r depends on longer-term developments in the world economy and on the course of economic policy in Germany and elsewhere, especially tax policy.

The second approach uses $Z'_t = (K_t - 1.021K_{t-1})/Y_{t-1}$ as the dependent variable:

$$Z'_t = \beta_0 + \beta_1 Z'_{t-1} + \beta_2 Z'_{t-2} + \beta_3 \frac{K_{t-1}}{Y_{t-1}} + e_t,$$

$\beta_0 = 0.21363$ (7.45783)
$\beta_1 = 0.70813$ (5.34050)
$\beta_2 = -0.40976$ (4.20902)
$\beta_3 = -0.10272$ (7.40101)

$R^2 = 0.9800$, $DW = 1.7711$.

The fit of this equation is shown in Chart 6-A1. In the steady state, $Z'_t = 0$. This implies that $K/Y = -\beta_0/\beta_3 = 2.08$ in the long run, an estimate that is consistent with those obtained earlier. A simpler version of this equation, which collapses the dynamics implied by the lagged dependent variables, was used in the simulations. The equation was also estimated for the period 1960–80, yielding an estimate of 2.05 for the steady-state capital-output ratio, relatively close to the current value (Chart 6-A1).[21]

---

[20]Using the estimates for β_2 and β_3 obtained from the equation that was not corrected for serial correlation yielded similar estimates: $r = 0.138$, $\psi = 0.00865$, and $K/Y = 2.29$, for the implied parameters.

[21]A casual inspection of the data seems to confirm the impression that the capital-output ratio is converging to a value somewhat greater than two. However, simply eyeballing the series can be misleading. In the late 1970s the ratio appeared to be converging to 1.9 and to 1.7 in the late 1960s.

Recent Occasional Papers of the International Monetary Fund

125. United Germany: The First Five Years—Performance and Policy Issues, by Robert Corker, Robert A. Feldman, Karl Habermeier, Hari Vittas, and Tessa van der Willigen. 1995.

124. Saving Behavior and the Asset Price "Bubble" in Japan: Analytical Studies, edited by Ulrich Baumgartner and Guy Meredith. 1995.

123. Comprehensive Tax Reform: The Colombian Experience, edited by Parthasarathi Shome. 1995.

122. Capital Flows in the APEC Region, edited by Mohsin S. Khan and Carmen M. Reinhart. 1995.

121. Uganda: Adjustment with Growth, 1987–94, by Robert L. Sharer, Hema R. De Zoysa, and Calvin A. McDonald. 1995.

120. Economic Dislocation and Recovery in Lebanon, by Sena Eken, Paul Cashin, S. Nuri Erbas, Jose Martelino, and Adnan Mazarei. 1995.

119. Singapore: A Case Study in Rapid Development, edited by Kenneth Bercuson with a staff team comprising Robert G. Carling, Aasim M. Husain, Thomas Rumbaugh, and Rachel van Elkan. 1995.

118. Sub-Saharan Africa: Growth, Savings, and Investment, by Michael T. Hadjimichael, Dhaneshwar Ghura, Martin Mühleisen, Roger Nord, and E. Murat Uçer. 1995.

117. Resilience and Growth Through Sustained Adjustment: The Moroccan Experience, by Saleh M. Nsouli, Sena Eken, Klaus Enders, Van-Can Thai, Jörg Decressin, and Filippo Cartiglia, with Janet Bungay. 1995.

116. Improving the International Monetary System: Constraints and Possibilities, by Michael Mussa, Morris Goldstein, Peter B. Clark, Donald J. Mathieson, and Tamim Bayoumi. 1994.

115. Exchange Rates and Economic Fundamentals: A Framework for Analysis, by Peter B. Clark, Leonardo Bartolini, Tamim Bayoumi, and Steven Symansky. 1994.

114. Economic Reform in China: A New Phase, by Wanda Tseng, Hoe Ee Khor, Kalpana Kochhar, Dubravko Mihaljek, and David Burton. 1994.

113. Poland: The Path to a Market Economy, by Liam P. Ebrill, Ajai Chopra, Charalambos Christofides, Paul Mylonas, Inci Otker, and Gerd Schwartz. 1994.

112. The Behavior of Non-Oil Commodity Prices, by Eduardo Borensztein, Mohsin S. Khan, Carmen M. Reinhart, and Peter Wickham. 1994.

111. The Russian Federation in Transition: External Developments, by Benedicte Vibe Christensen. 1994.

110. Limiting Central Bank Credit to the Government: Theory and Practice, by Carlo Cottarelli. 1993.

109. The Path to Convertibility and Growth: The Tunisian Experience, by Saleh M. Nsouli, Sena Eken, Paul Duran, Gerwin Bell, and Zühtü Yücelik. 1993.

108. Recent Experiences with Surges in Capital Inflows, by Susan Schadler, Maria Carkovic, Adam Bennett, and Robert Kahn. 1993.

107. China at the Threshold of a Market Economy, by Michael W. Bell, Hoe Ee Khor, and Kalpana Kochhar with Jun Ma, Simon N'guiamba, and Rajiv Lall. 1993.

106. Economic Adjustment in Low-Income Countries: Experience Under the Enhanced Structural Adjustment Facility, by Susan Schadler, Franek Rozwadowski, Siddharth Tiwari, and David O. Robinson. 1993.

105. The Structure and Operation of the World Gold Market, by Gary O'Callaghan. 1993.

104. Price Liberalization in Russia: Behavior of Prices, Household Incomes, and Consumption During the First Year, by Vincent Koen and Steven Phillips. 1993.

103. Liberalization of the Capital Account: Experiences and Issues, by Donald J. Mathieson and Liliana Rojas-Suárez. 1993.

102. Financial Sector Reforms and Exchange Arrangements in Eastern Europe. Part I: Financial Markets and Intermediation, by Guillermo A. Calvo and Manmohan S. Kumar. Part II: Exchange Arrangements of Previously Centrally Planned Economies, by Eduardo Borensztein and Paul R. Masson. 1993.

101. Spain: Converging with the European Community, by Michel Galy, Gonzalo Pastor, and Thierry Pujol. 1993.

100. The Gambia: Economic Adjustment in a Small Open Economy, by Michael T. Hadjimichael, Thomas Rumbaugh, and Eric Verreydt. 1992.

99. Mexico: The Strategy to Achieve Sustained Economic Growth, edited by Claudio Loser and Eliot Kalter. 1992.

98. Albania: From Isolation Toward Reform, by Mario I. Blejer, Mauro Mecagni, Ratna Sahay, Richard Hides, Barry Johnston, Piroska Nagy, and Roy Pepper. 1992.

97. Rules and Discretion in International Economic Policy, by Manuel Guitián. 1992.

96. Policy Issues in the Evolving International Monetary System, by Morris Goldstein, Peter Isard, Paul R. Masson, and Mark P. Taylor. 1992.

95. The Fiscal Dimensions of Adjustment in Low-Income Countries, by Karim Nashashibi, Sanjeev Gupta, Claire Liuksila, Henri Lorie, and Walter Mahler. 1992.

94. Tax Harmonization in the European Community: Policy Issues and Analysis, edited by George Kopits. 1992.

93. Regional Trade Arrangements, by Augusto de la Torre and Margaret R. Kelly. 1992.

92. Stabilization and Structural Reform in the Czech and Slovak Federal Republic: First Stage, by Bijan B. Aghevli, Eduardo Borensztein, and Tessa van der Willigen. 1992.

91. Economic Policies for a New South Africa, edited by Desmond Lachman and Kenneth Bercuson with a staff team comprising Daudi Ballali, Robert Corker, Charalambos Christofides, and James Wein. 1992.

90. The Internationalization of Currencies: An Appraisal of the Japanese Yen, by George S. Tavlas and Yuzuru Ozeki. 1992.

89. The Romanian Economic Reform Program, by Dimitri G. Demekas and Mohsin S. Khan. 1991.

88. Value-Added Tax: Administrative and Policy Issues, edited by Alan A. Tait. 1991.

87. Financial Assistance from Arab Countries and Arab Regional Institutions, by Pierre van den Boogaerde. 1991.

86. Ghana: Adjustment and Growth, 1983–91, by Ishan Kapur, Michael T. Hadjimichael, Paul Hilbers, Jerald Schiff, and Philippe Szymczak. 1991.

85. Thailand: Adjusting to Success—Current Policy Issues, by David Robinson, Yangho Byeon, and Ranjit Teja with Wanda Tseng. 1991.

84. Financial Liberalization, Money Demand, and Monetary Policy in Asian Countries, by Wanda Tseng and Robert Corker. 1991.

83. Economic Reform in Hungary Since 1968, by Anthony R. Boote and Janos Somogyi. 1991.

82. Characteristics of a Successful Exchange Rate System, by Jacob A. Frenkel, Morris Goldstein, and Paul R. Masson. 1991.

81. Currency Convertibility and the Transformation of Centrally Planned Economies, by Joshua E. Greene and Peter Isard. 1991.

80. Domestic Public Debt of Externally Indebted Countries, by Pablo E. Guidotti and Manmohan S. Kumar. 1991.

79. The Mongolian People's Republic: Toward a Market Economy, by Elizabeth Milne, John Leimone, Franek Rozwadowski, and Padej Sukachevin. 1991.

78. Exchange Rate Policy in Developing Countries: Some Analytical Issues, by Bijan B. Aghevli, Mohsin S. Khan, and Peter J. Montiel. 1991.

77. Determinants and Systemic Consequences of International Capital Flows, by Morris Goldstein, Donald J. Mathieson, David Folkerts-Landau, Timothy Lane, J. Saúl Lizondo, and Liliana Rojas-Suárez. 1991.

76. China: Economic Reform and Macroeconomic Management, by Mario Blejer, David Burton, Steven Dunaway, and Gyorgy Szapary. 1991.

75. German Unification: Economic Issues, edited by Leslie Lipschitz and Donogh McDonald. 1990.

74. The Impact of the European Community's Internal Market on the EFTA, by Richard K. Abrams, Peter K. Cornelius, Per L. Hedfors, and Gunnar Tersman. 1990.

73. The European Monetary System: Developments and Perspectives, by Horst Ungerer, Jouko J. Hauvonen, Augusto Lopez-Claros, and Thomas Mayer. 1990.

Note: For information on the title and availability of Occasional Papers not listed, please consult the IMF Publications Catalog or contact IMF Publication Services.